F-86 SABRE
FIGHTER-BOMBER
UNITS OVER KOREA

OSPREY AVIATION

OSPREY FRONTLINE COLOUR

2

F-86 SABRE
FIGHTER-BOMBER
UNITS OVER KOREA

Warren Thompson

First published in Great Britain in 1999 by Osprey Publishing,
1st Floor Elms Court, Chapel Way, Botley, Oxford, OX2 9LP

ISBN 1 85532 929 8

Edited by Tony Holmes
Page design by Ken Vail Graphic Design, Cambridge, UK
Cutaway Drawing by Mike Badrocke

Printed in Hong Kong

FRONT COVER *An impressive line-up of brand new F-86F fighter-
bombers at Suwon AB during the summer of 1953. The nearest
Sabre to the camera was assigned to the CO of the 8th Fighter
Bomber Wing (FBW), as indicated by the multi-coloured sunbursts
painted on the jet's vertical stabiliser – these represented all three
squadrons within the Wing. The blue-tailed Sabres behind the CO's
F-86 all hailed from the 35th Fighter Bomber Squadron (FBS). The
8th FBW was unique in that it had flown three aircraft types
during the Korean War, namely the F-51, F-80 and, finally, the F-86
(James Carter)*

BACK COVER *Lt Sam Harris poses in front of his F-86F at Suwon.
His blue helmet and the similar-coloured trim on the Sabre behind
him denote that they were assigned to the 35th FBS of the 8th
FBW. This squadron was the second unit within the wing to give up
its F-80Cs and convert to the new Sabres, commencing the
transition on 14 March 1953. At that time, all of the remaining
F-80s within the wing were moved over to the 80th FBS, which
would duly become the last fighter-bomber squadron to fly the
Shooting Star in the Korean War (Sam Harris)*

TITLE PAGE *Very few, if any, of the 36th FBS Sabres escaped
having names written on both the left and right sides of the
fuselage. FU-399 Irish's Shillelagh was no exception, with its pilot,
Lt Lloyd Irish, being one of the original Sabre pilots drafted into
the squadron during its transition to the North American fighter in
the early spring of 1953. The 8th FBW's aircraft were parked on
the east side of Suwon, and the west side was occupied by the
high-scoring 51st FIW, which was solely involved in performing the
interceptor mission (Lloyd Irish)*

TITLE VERSO PAGE *All pilots that transitioned onto any type of jet
in Korea had to go through ejection seat training at Taegu AB
(K-2). As this photograph clearly shows, the pilot got to experience
what it would be like to vacate an F-86 in flight using the North
American Aviation T-4E ejection seat fitted to the F-model Sabre.
The only sensation that could not be reproduced in this
demonstration were the forces that hit you when you ejected at
high speed. The 'two-and-a-half' F-84E Thunderjets sharing the
open-ended hangar with the ejection seat rig belonged to the
9th FBS/49th FBW (Kenneth Koon)*

EDITOR'S NOTE

To make the new *Osprey Frontline Colour* series as authoritative
as possible, the editor would be interested in hearing from any
individual who may have relevant information relating to the
aircraft/units/pilots featured in this, or any other, volume
published by Osprey Aviation. Similarly, comments on the
editorial content of this book would also be most welcome.
Please write to Tony Holmes at 10 Prospect Road, Sevenoaks,
Kent, TN13 3UA, Great Britain, or e-mail tony.holmes@osprey-
jets.freeserve.co.uk

For a catalogue of all books published by Osprey Military,
Aviation and Automotive please write to:

**The Marketing Manager, Osprey Publishing
Limited, PO Box 140, Wellingborough, Northants
NN8 4ZA, United Kingdom
Email:info@OspreyDirect.co.uk**

**Osprey Direct USA, P.O Box 130, Sterling Heights,
MI 48311-0130, USA
Email:info@OspreyDirectUSA.com**

OR VISIT OUR WEBSITE AT
http://www.osprey-publishing.co.uk

Contents

LEFT *Two anonymous 12th FBS pilots enjoy their time out of the cockpit as they relax on a pair of 500-lb bombs that are waiting to be loaded onto an aircraft. Behind the men, a group of officers clutching cameras have gathered around F-86F FU-323, although the exact reason for this congregation has been lost over the intervening decades. FU-323 was shot down on 16 June 1953 while initiating a dive-bomb attack on an enemy truck, its pilot, Lt James H Allston, being killed in the subsequent crash. Mid-June 1953 was a particularly brutal time for the 12th FBS (William Barber)*

CHAPTER ONE
BACKGROUND

The Korean War lasted for exactly 37 months and two days, and it proved to be one of the bloodiest conflicts the United States has ever been involved in. Howver, the massive loss of life sustained by the forces of the United Nations (UN) in their attempt to stop the spread of communism into South Korea had little impact on an American public still 'war-weary' from World War 2.

This lack of interest in the Korean conflict was duly reflected in the media coverage the war received at the time. In many respects, this still exists today, with the first real struggle between communism and democracy having been consigned to the history books as 'the forgotten war'.

The Korean War was different in many respects from World War 2, which had been fought just a decade earlier. Granted, ground troops still travelled primarily on foot, and tanks and artillery were still deciding factors in the numerous battles that were fought between the Pusan Perimeter and the Yalu River. However, one of the most influential weapons of war in the 20th century reached new levels of sophistication over the battlefields

of Korea. Its 'infancy' had spanned World War 1 and its 'adolescence' the six years from 1939 through to 1945. By the time of the Korean War, it had reached full maturity. This weapon was airpower.

The air war over Korea not only encompassed aerial combat as seen in the past. It also ushered in the new era of the jet, and the revised tactics that went along with them. Finally, close air support was developed to a degree that could never have been imagined in the past.

The first fighter-bombers to see combat in Korea were far from jet-powered, however, taking the form of World War 2-vintage F-51 Mustangs, F4U Corsairs and postwar F-82 Twin Mustangs. The jet age entered this realm with the F-80 Shooting Star, F-84 Thunderjet and F9F Panther just weeks into the conflict. All of these types would go on to achieve a high degree of success in the close air support and interdiction roles.

As the war entered the autumn of 1950, and UN forces had all but defeated the North Korean People's Army (NKPA), the only significant communist targets that remained untouched were situated in the north of the

LEFT *By the spring of 1953, any communist assets of note near the frontline had been surrounded by sophisticated Chinese flak batteries. This meant that attacking these targets with 'low and slow' fighter-bombers was akin to committing suicide, so the task of neutralising them was left to the newly-arrived F-86F, which could rely on its speed to outpace the flak. However, as this shot shows, even the Sabre was not immune to AAA. Wearing the yellow sunburst tail marking of the 80th FBS at Suwon (K-13), FU-434 is the object of much amazement for two squadron groundcrew sent to inspect the damage (Robert Odle)*

battle-scarred country, near the Yalu River – and directly opposite Manchuria. With various USAF units moving north to operate more closely with the troops 'on the ground', and the enemy in full retreat, it certainly appeared that the Korean War would indeed be 'over by Christmas'. However, on 26 November 1950, the Chinese Army sprung into action, pitching 100,000 troops into battle across the Yalu River. From that moment on, it became a completely different war, and one that would drag on for another 32 tortuous months.

By March 1951, the B-29 bombers committed to the war had completely destroyed every target that Bomber Command had considered 'strategic'. Indeed, the number of UN aircraft in-theatre had become so overwhelming that the Chinese stopped trying to move their supplies, or troops, during daylight hours.

During 1951-52, the fighter-bombers logged tens of thousands of sorties all over the North Korean segment of the peninsula. And while there were no obvious targets now moving during the day, they 'worked over' known enemy troops concentrations, railroads, airfields and major road intersections. Although pilots could not make 'eye contact' with the enemy on the ground, they exerted much effort and energy into making it all but impossible for the communists' logistics requirement to be met. Thus, numerous major enemy offensives were delayed, or cancelled, because of the fighter-bombers.

For much of the Korean War the F-84 Thunderjet was the fighter-bomber of choice, being the best close air

support aircraft in the USAF inventory. Indeed, it could be compared both in terms of its design and role to a subsequent product from the Republic stable which would become the staple American fighter-bomber in yet another struggle against communism, this time over South-east Asia, a little more than a decade later – the F-105 Thunderchief. Both aircraft could absorb a lot of punishment and still get their ordnance over the target. They could also bring their pilots back safely.

Aside from the F-84, the USAF's other primary fighter-bomber types were the F-51 and F-80. Both aircraft shouldered far more responsibility in the Korean War than they should have, with much of the early fighter-bomber work falling to the obsolescent Shooting Star simply because it was readily available in large numbers throughout the Far East Air Force (FEAF) when the war began.

Weary F-51s also filled a serious gap in UN ranks early on because the airfields in South Korea were so crude that jets could not operate in such conditions (see *Osprey Frontline Colour 1 – F-51 Mustang Units over Korea* for further details). Most examples of the AAF's classic fighter of World War 2 had been retired from the front-line by the summer of 1950, forcing the USAF to hastily (and embarrassingly) 'raid' Air National Guards units across America for Mustangs to send to the frontline in Korea. The F-51 subsequently 'held the line' until sufficient numbers of F-84s had begun to appear in-theatre.

The arrival of the Thunderjets allowed the surviving

Mustangs and Shooting Stars to be gradually phased out of the FEAF, although the rate at which they were replaced can be gauged by the fact that both types were still flying combat missions over Korea in early 1953.

At their peak in the autumn of 1950, Mustangs and Shooting Stars equipped a total of five fighter bomber wings – the 18th and 35th flew F-51Ds, the 49th and 51st operated the F-80C, and the 8th flew a mixed force of both types. However, with the arrival of more modern jets, surviving Mustangs and Shooting Stars were funnelled to an ever-shrinking list of users. The 35th FBW transferred out of Korea in May 1951 (leaving their few remaining F-51Ds to the 18th FBW), the 49th converted onto the F-84 just weeks later, and the 51st moved into the fighter interceptor role in the late summer of that same year with the arrival of new F-86Es.

However, the remaining 8th and 18th FBWs stayed loyal to the F-80C and F-51D, respectively, into the spring of 1953. This established both types as 'prime movers' in close air support and interdiction. The Mustang, in particular, had suffered heavy losses to ground fire during its time in the frontline, the aircraft's liquid-cooled Packard-Merlin engine proving less than robust in the face of flak and small arms fire. Rising attrition eventually meant that the two Mustang squadrons operated by the 8th FBW had to turn their few surviving mounts over to the 18th FBW, receiving more F-80Cs in their place.

As previously mentioned, as the war ground on the F-84 Thunderjet eventually became the numerically dominant fighter-bomber in-theatre, although the F-51 still had a major presence over the battlefield – especially against road and rail targets all the way north to Pyongyang.

MiGS OVER THE YALU

The entry of the Russian-built MiG-15 in early November 1950 had a dramatic impact on the fighter-bombers, and their areas of responsibility. Previously, F-51s had been able to roam freely virtually anywhere in Korea. However, the MiG fighter posed a great threat to their survival, so the vast majority of deep penetration missions north to the Yalu River region were passed over to the newly-arrived F-84s in December. Although the latter enjoyed

BELOW *Most of the major airbases in South Korea were frequently visited by the USO troops, and in this shot, two girls from the touring party are seen being given a first class tour of a 12th FBS Sabre by pilot, Lt George Anderson (William Barber)*

additional protection on these sorties from equally new F-86As, the Thunderjet pilots were also capable of defending themselves, and several kills were claimed over the MiG-15s. F-80Cs were also sent on missions that were considered to be within the range of the MiGs, but unlike the F-84s or F-86s, the Lockheed jet was no match for the Soviet-built fighter.

As the war moved into its third year (June/July 1952), FEAF, and the top UN military planners in-theatre, had a decision to make. The older fighter-bombers still operated by two major wings in Korea were in dire need of replacement. It had already been decided that the 18th FBW would move further north from Chinhae (K-10) to its staging base at Hoengsong (K-46), thus cutting down the levels of in-transit 'wear and tear' inflicted on the Wing's F-51s whilst shuttling to and from the frontline.

When looking for a replacement fighter-bomber, FEAF senior officers had certainly been made aware of the versatility of the Sabre. Indeed, during May 1952, tests had been undertaken with the combat-seasoned 4th Fighter Interceptor Wing (FIW) at Kimpo AB (K-14), using modified F-86E-10s configured as fighter-bombers –

bombs were affixed to the single underwing pylons in place of the external tanks. Some of the missions flown were undertaken by seasoned fighter pilot, and multiple-kill World War 2 ace, Col Walker M 'Bud' Mahurin, who was then CO of the 4th FIG.

Several of the sorties flown saw jets fitted with 1000-lb Mk 84 GP bombs, and the results showed the immense potential of the Sabre in this role. On one of the missions, specially-rigged fighter-bombers attacked the airfields at Sinuiju and Uiju, and scored precision hits with the 'thousand pounders'. They were also successful against marshalling yards at Kunu-ri, and it was during one such attack on this target on 13 May that Col Mahurin was shot down by heavy ground fire and made a PoW.

As a result of studying the statistics compiled during these test missions, the USAF determined that the Sabre had a brilliant future in this new role. On 18 July 1952, orders were 'cut' to the effect that both the 8th and 18th FBWs would convert over to the new F-86F (with its new engine, '6-3 hard wing' and additional wing pylons) fighter-bomber as soon as North American's production line could churn out sufficient aircraft to equip both

LEFT *The arrival of new F-86Fs at Osan drew a lot of attention from members of the 18th FBW. Dozens of cameras appeared on the flightline, and everyone had their picture taken standing by the new aircraft. Facing the camera in this photograph is Lt Michael Encinias, who is wearing his yellow baseball cap to denote his allegiance to the 12th FBS. The yellow nose on the aircraft behind him also marks out this factory-fresh F-86F as being part of the 'Foxy Few'. The 12th was the first squadron to stand down for conversion onto the new fighter-bomber Sabres (William Barber)*

FAR LEFT TOP *Down time meant quality time to the 67th FBS, for they had their own 'Red Scarf' club on the base at Osan. Most of the off-duty pilots gathered here to discuss missions, and numerous other matters of crucial importance to a jet pilot in Korea. Osan was situated in the middle of the country's rural 'heart', and there was absolutely nothing to do off-base. Therefore, this facility was often the site of large parties, with all the 'guests' wearing standard-issue 67th FBS red baseball caps! (Robert Niklaus)*

FAR LEFT BOTTOM *A flight of 67th FBS F-86Fs return from a mission over North Korea. This photograph was taken at low-level in the vicinity of Osan AB just prior to the pilots working into the landing pattern. The 67th was the last USAF squadron to fly the F-51 in combat, completing numerous missions in January 1953 from both Chinhae and Osan whilst the rest of the 18th FBW made their move to the new 'super' base at the latter site (Dwight Lee)*

The avionics and ordnance specialists at Osan were constantly working within the complicated confines of the F-model's nose. This side view of a 67th FBS Sabre was taken whilst the aircraft was safely parked within the confines of its blast revetment. The long-range drop tanks synonymous with Sabre operations in Korea can be seen plumbed under the wings of the jet, although it is presently devoid of ordnance (James Gregg)

RIGHT *The maintenance squadrons in Korea became close knit units as the war dragged on, with the ultimate goal for these outfits being a ramp full of F-86s 'good to go' at any given time. The men seen in this photograph are from the 67th FBS's 'A' Flight at Osan. The percentage figure for aircraft available for operations during the summer of 1953 was consistently very high, and this allowed squadrons to satisfy the great demand for Sabre fighter-bombers over the frontline (Don Whicker).*

FAR RIGHT *These three 0.50-cal machine guns provided half of the F-86F's integral firepower. The Colt-Browning weapons were the key to an effective high-angle strafing run or a successful engagement with a MiG-15. Indeed, while the job of a Sabre fighter-bomber was to 'haul bombs and move mud', the F-86F was more than capable of taking on any aircraft the communist forces should put up to deflect them from carrying out their primary role. This Sabre was assigned to the 80th FBS 'Headhunters' at Suwon (Robert Odle)*

wings. Initially, the target date set for introduction of the new aircraft was mid-November 1952, and this date proved to be crucial, for MiG-15 units were now trying out new tactics that saw them employing drop tanks. These allowed the communist fighter pilots to range further south into airspace used by F-51Ds and F-80Cs.

Granted, the MiG pilots were flying at extremely high altitudes whilst 'down south', remaining well above the vulnerable fighter-bombers. However, their use of external tanks was allowing them to employ 'pincer' tactic in order to catch fuel-critical F-84s returning south after flying deep penetration sorties. The arrival of new F-86Fs meant that the MiGs would have their hands full if they 'jumped' returning fighter-bombers. Indeed, the F-model proved to be such a worthy opponent for the communist fighter that it did not require a dedicated escort to protect it.

By mid-April 1953, FEAF aircraft had completed no fewer than 732,350 sorties. The bombers and fighter-

bombers had destroyed 74,864 vehicles, 9898 railcars/locomotives and 1200 Soviet-built T-34 tanks, and inflicted over 180,000 enemy troop casualties. These bold statistics make for impressive reading, but they had been achieved at a high price. Of the 725 UN aircraft lost during 34 months of combat, 619 were fighter-bombers. And it had been the age old enemy of the fighter-bomber that had been the lethal killer of aircraft – accurate and intense ground fire, not the MiG-15.

At about the time that the FEAF was releasing these figures, F-86F fighter-bombers were achieving full operability in Korea with the 8th and 18th FBWs. While their contribution to the war effort spanned just a few short months, their operations had a resounding effect on close support and interdiction tactics for many years to come. For what was learned by pilots flying the nimble F-86F over Korea was passed on to those units sent to Vietnam in the legendary F-100 Super Sabre just 12 years later.

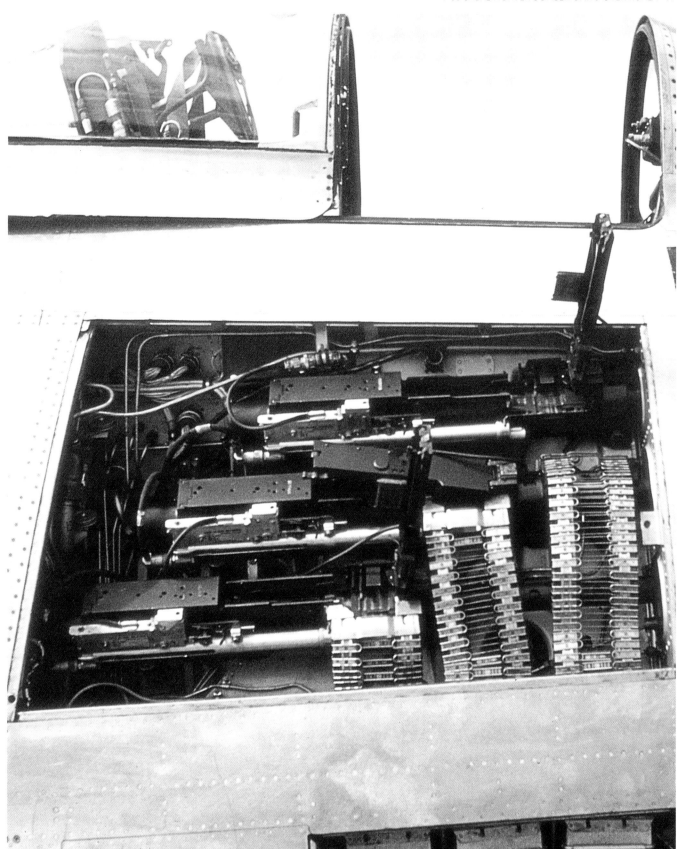

ABOVE *Engine changes were the most complicated and time consuming of all the maintenance procedures undertaken at the forward bases, with the peak number carried out in a single month being ten in June 1953. Ground fires and loose objects sucked off dusty taxyways were the main causes of engine failure. Seen here lacking various panels and its tail section, PUDDY TAT was assigned to the 12th FBS (Dick Kempthorne)*

RIGHT *No 2 Sqn of the South African Air Force was attached to the 18th FBW throughtout the Korean War, converting from the Mustang to the Sabre at the same time as the two USAF squadrons within the wing. This shot of a South African F-86F recovering at Osan was taken in the summer of 1953 (Dwight Lee)*

RIGHT *Lt Cliff Nunnery gives a sense of scale to 'bunker-busting' 1000-lb GP bombs. The F-86F could rapidly carry two of these devices to any target in North Korea. Aerial refuelling was not an option for the Sabre in 1953, so the external tanks synonymous with the jet had to get it to the target, leaving the internal fuel to bring the pilot home. The primary difference between the F-80 and the F-86 in the fighter-bomber role was that the latter aircraft spent scant seconds in 'harm's way' over the target. The adage of 'speed is life' was never more true than for the fighter-bomber pilots over Korea (Cliff Nunnery)*

BELOW RIGHT *The top 'MiG killer' in the fighter-bomber fraternity was Maj James Hagerstrom, CO of the 67th FBS. His aerial prowess in the Sabre had been developed long before he went into the bomber business, and he made no attempt to hide the fact that his primary interest was air-to-air combat. This photograph shows 67th FBS pilot Lt Robert Cassatt posing in front of Hagerstrom's F-86F "MIG POISON" (which bears 6.5 red stars on its canopy rail) at Osan in the early summer of 1953 (Robert Cassatt)*

FAR RIGHT *A classic view of a 'Head Hunter' Sabre on patrol over South Korea, close to the 38th Parallel. The yellow sunburst tails were the trademark of the 80th FBS, which was the last F-80C squadron to swap over to the new fighter-bomber (Raymond Lee)*

One of the more colourful Sabres assigned to the 67th FBS was DENNIS THE MENACE, which was named after the popular cartoon strip then being published in Sunday newspapers across the United States. Such ties with home were never broken, regardless of how far away 'home' may have seemed to the Sabre crews. Although originally named DENNIS THE MENACE – for obvious reasons – by its first pilot, Maj Dennis Clark, the jet had been passed to Lt Reid Ivins by the time this photograph was taken in November 1953 (B R Kibort)

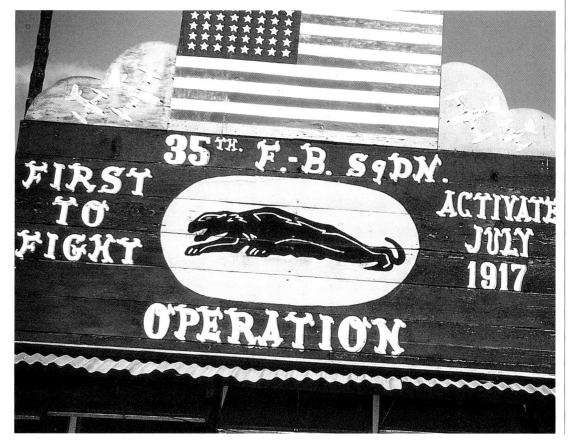

FAR LEFT *A group of 80th FBS pilots show an interest in an ejection seat that has been removed from one of their Sabres. This apparatus was one of the most important features of any jet fighter, for it greatly enhanced the pilot's chances of survival should his aircraft be hit by flak, or by a well-aimed burst of cannon fire from a MiG-15. This shot was taken at Suwon AB, home of the 8th FBW (Robert Odle)*

TOP LEFT *A good frontal view of a 67th FBS Sabre parked out on the ramp at Osan AB (K-55). During the final three days of the war, both Sabre fighter-bomber wings were involved in a massive attempt to crater the runways of every known airbase in North Korea, for communist forces were trying their best to make sure that they had aircraft based south of the Yalu River when the ceasefire was signed. That would enable them to keep the aeroplanes in North Korea postwar, for the treaty banned the importation of any further military hardware once the ceasefire had come into effect (Robert Niklaus)*

BOTTOM LEFT *All of the squadrons that flew the F-86F in the bomber role had outstanding combat records that dated back to before World War 2. As noted in this sign (seen affixed to the roof of the 35th FBS's Operations Building at Suwon in the summer of 1953), this unit could trace its lineage to World War 1 (Marvin Patton)*

INSET The only squadron that did not use an official emblem during the fighter-bomber era of the Korean War was the 12th FBS. Instead, its personnel chose to keep the 'Foxy Few' logo that had been created soon after the unit had arrived in Korea from Clark AFB, in the Philippines, in July 1950. The emblem had been designed by legendary Mustang pilots 'Spud' Taylor and 'Chappie' James, and this particular rendition was posted on the 12th's Operations Building at Osan (Gene Buttyan)

MAIN PICTURE The transition from a piston-engined fighter to a state-of-the-art jet was a serious undertaking that did not always go entirely to plan, as this photograph clearly shows – this 12th FBS Sabre was involved in a landing accident at Osan. Note the rarely seen marking on the jet's vertical stabiliser, which the 18th FBW had initially adopted, before being ordered by the FEAF to switch to the now familiar red, white and blue chevrons (Bill Juhrs)

CHAPTER 2

CONVERSION TO THE F-86F

BELOW *The first F-86F to be delivered to the 18th FBW at Osan was hastily decorated in South African Air Force markings soon after its arrival. It drew a large crowd, as many of the enlisted personnel within the wing had never previously seen a Sabre up close. Despite carrying the distinctive Springbok roundel, this aircraft was soon assigned to the 12th FBS, which was the first unit within the wing to convert from the Mustang to the F-86F. This photograph was taken in early 1953, several weeks before any of the 18th FBW's squadrons became operational (Francis Swartz)*

The FEAF had decided from the beginning that the 18th FBW would get the new F-86F first. Their F-51Ds were the oldest, slowest and weariest fighter-bombers in Korea, so their priority was justified. However, the wing had been operating from crude airfields at Chinhae (K-10) and Hoengsong (K-46), and neither base was in any fit shape to accommodate jet aircraft. Therefore, before any conversion could take place, a new base had to be found for the trio of squadrons that comprised the wing. Thanks to advanced planning by the FEAF, however, a suitable site was chosen and no real delays were experienced.

With the first F-86F-30s already slated to go to the 18th FBW, a further directive issued by the controlling Fifth Air Force on 15 December 1952 confirmed that the wing would move to a new 'super base' that was almost

ready for occupation. The facility was called Osan (K-55), and the move had to be completed by no later than 31 December 1952. Of course, very few things this complex ever go according to plan, and unsurprisingly, the new base remained unfinished come the last day of 1952. And even if it had been ready for operations on time, the 18th FBW had still not received its first F-86Fs, despite an original conversion date of mid-November!

Preparation for this monumental base shift and aircraft swap finally commenced on 29 December when the F-86-11 Mobile Training Unit (MTU) began arriving at Osan. Everything was in place by 7 January, the unit having been brought over from Chanute AFB, in Illinois. At this time, the 18th FBW was still involved in flying a steady programme of combat missions out of its forward base at

Hoengsong (K-46), using three squadrons to fulfil its obligations, namely the 12th and 67th FBS, and the South African Air Force's No 2 Sqn.

The 12th would give up their Mustangs first, standing down from combat on 8 January 1953 and flying their F-51Ds back to Kisarazu AB, Japan, by way of Itazuke AB.

The 18th FBW's radical change in operational equipment provided the USAF with several 'firsts', for not only was a frontline combat outfit converting from a propeller-driven aircraft to a state-of-the-art jet, it was doing so at a forward base under combat conditions. To add a further dimension to the swap over, that forward base was new to the wing, and the FEAF as a whole, and was incomplete. Finally, to top it all off, the entire process was being carried out in the depths of a typically harsh Korean winter.

With the 12th FBS 'hitting the manuals' by early January 1953, the South Africans became the next unit to stand down. This left just the 67th FBS at K-46, flying as many missions as it could handle with all of the wing's surviving F-51Ds.

On 15 January the 67th launched its last major strike out of Hoengsong, the F-51s then recovering at Osan AB.

This was a significant event in the history of the 18th FBW, for less than a week later (23 January 1953, to be precise), the 67th FBS flew its last combat mission of the war with the F-51D. The unit was then officially removed from the available frontline force.

According to official records kept by the wing, 20 Mustangs were flown back to Japan on 17 January, with the remaining 26 fighters flying out from Osan 11 days later. The retirement of the legendary World War 2-vintage fighter from the USAF's frontline force was carried out with very little fanfare from the media. Indeed, the significance of the event was only truly realised within the ranks of the 18th FBW itself.

No 2 SQN SAAF

The South African-manned No 2 Sqn revelled in its reputation for both fighting and 'playing' hard! In fact so much of the latter was done out of the cockpit that many of the surviving pilots from the 18th FBW's two remaining squadrons are still curious to this day as to when their South African compatriots found the time to sleep.

ABOVE *During the 18th FBW's intense transition period, the wing borrowed several T-33s from the F-84 squadrons based at Kunsan and Taegu ABs. Their employment meant that more pilots could be checked out over a shorter period of time, and they also allowed an instructor to accompany a piston-engined pilot on his first few jet sorties. Once all three squadrons within the wing had transitioned to the F-86, each unit was assigned it own T-33 for the training of new pilots that rotated in at periodic intervals. This aircraft was seen at Osan in the summer of 1953 (Kenneth Koon)*

The exploits of No 2 Sqn during the Mustang era are legendary. Final figures from official SAAF records state that 95 Mustangs were bought from the USAF, and of this total, no fewer than 74 of them were lost to all causes – the human cost of these losses was 34 pilots listed as either killed or missing in action. These statistics make for grim reading, and the 12th and 67th FBSs suffered similar casualties both in terms of men and machinery, such was the nature of the fighter-bomber mission.

No 2 Sqn had logged 2890 missions and 10,597 sorties on the F-51 by the time the unit flew its 22 remaining Mustangs to Kisarazu AB on 31 December 1952. Concurrently with retiring their veteran piston-engined fighters, the squadron reported to K-55 for transition onto the F-86F.

One of the first problems faced by the wing following the retirement of the F-51 was what to do with the many high-time Mustang pilots that populated the trio of squadrons within its charge. The process of retraining and then 'checking out' pilots in the Sabre was very costly, and if the USAF could not get a certain number of missions from a pilot after he had completed the training regimen,

then he was considered to be a poor investment. Therefore, it was decided that any Mustang pilot that had flown less than 50 missions in Korea had to transition onto the Sabre, regardless of how he felt about shifting from a piston- to jet-engined fighter.

Those with a mission tally in excess of 50 would be dealt with on an individual basis. There were 29 such pilots within the 12th and 67th FBSs, and eight of them were removed from the frontline, whilst the remaining 21 transferred out of the wing to other assignments. In the majority of cases, the latter pilots finished their tours flying T-6s with the 'Mosquito' units, acting as Forward Air Controllers (FAC). There were exceptions, however, and a small number of the 'top timers' in Mustangs converted over to the F-86 and signed up for an extension to their tours.

The 8th FBW observed a similar policy at Suwon AB (K-13) when it commenced conversion onto the F-86F several weeks after the 18th had completed its aircraft/base 'swap'. As its squadrons stood down, the high-time F-80C pilots simply shifted over to a sister squadron that was still operational with the Shooting Star.

RIGHT *Wearing the early tail markings initially adopted by the 18th FBW, this aircraft is seen being towed to the gunnery range for bore-sighting at Osan during the first weeks of the 67th FBS's conversion onto the F-86F. The red trim above and below the blue star-spangled band on the aircraft's fin denotes the Sabre's allegiance to the 67th FBS (Francis Swartz)*

The 36th FBS was the first to 'check out' in the new Sabre, beginning this process on 22 February 1953. Accordingly, their 50+ mission types moved to the 35th or 80th FBSs. When the 35th commenced its transition on 14 March, its 'top timers' passed over to the 80th FBS 'Head Hunters' in order to finish off their combat tours.

The 8th FBW enjoyed a much smoother conversion onto the Sabre than the 18th due to its near-three years of jet experience with the F-80C. The schedule observed by the 18th FBW also called for the entire wing to be shut down at the same time, effectively displacing many of its pilots. The 8th, on the other hand, enjoyed the luxury of letting its pilots finish tours in aircraft they had grown accustomed to.

CONVERSION PROBLEMS

The MTU was overloaded at K-55. Classroom instruction ran for eight hours a day, seven days a week, and as many as three classes per day were being conducted by the instructors. With the war going on, UN forces could ill afford to have two full wings removed from the frontline for any great period of time. Therefore, the FEAF placed

great importance on getting the changeover completed in the shortest possible time, and thus hopefully minimising the number of combat sorties lost.

The pilots were not the only ones making the change, for their efforts over the frontline had to be fully supported by groundcrews, maintenance personnel and mission planners back at base. Indeed, before the 18th FBW could be deemed combat-ready with the F-86F, some 240 mechanics and mission specialists had to first be trained. In addition to these support personnel, the MTU also converted a total of 99 pilots onto the Sabre.

Three new F-86F-30s arrived at K-55 on 28 January 1953, and they were immediately issued to the 12th FBS. From this point onwards, a steady stream of factory-fresh Sabres were delivered to Osan until, on 31 March, the squadron had received the last of its 25 aircraft. Staggeringly, within a week both No 2 Sqn and the 67th FBS could also boast their full complement of new 'Dash-30s'!

With the arrival of aircraft, and the completion of the classroom work, pilots at last found themselves ready to strap into the Sabres and become proficient at what they

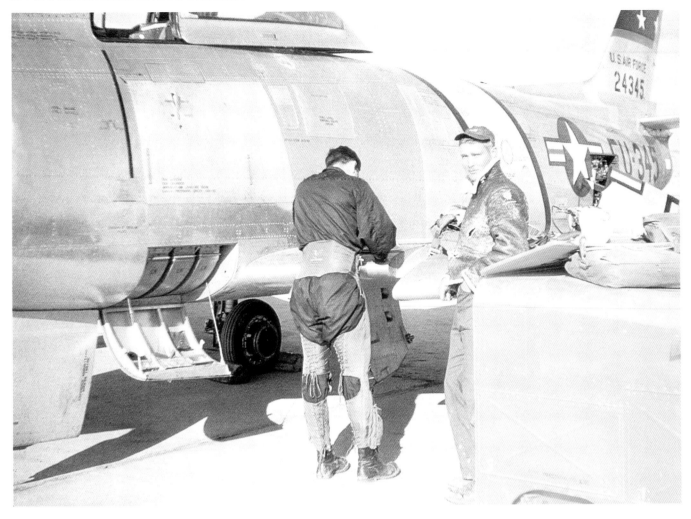

were paid to do – bomb and strafe the enemy. And unlike their more famous fighter interceptor brethren, 18th FBW pilots had to have a sound understanding of how best to use the F-86F as both a fighter and a bomber, for they were more than likely to encounter MiG-15s once back in the frontline.

The teaching of these skills to regular wing pilots was the primary mission of the Combat Crew Training Flight (CCTF), which was comprised of experienced instructors. For the 18th FBW, the original members of this elite group (set up on 1 January 1953) were Capt Howard Ebersole and Maj James Hagerstrom, who served as the first two flight instructors, and Maintenance Officer Lt George Reimer. These men were vested with the responsibility of checking out each pilot, no matter what his rank, and preparing him for combat.

The regimen involved in this phase was the same for both wings. The first item on the list was for each pilot to take his F-86 Pilot's Operation Manual (nicknamed the 'Dash-One') and sit with it in the cockpit of his new jet for a minimum of four hours, memorising everything in the cockpit. They were also encouraged to take a fellow pilot out with them to the jet in order to quiz each other on its various procedures. A combination of the two exercises was deemed the best way to become proficient enough to pass the blindfold cockpit check, which each pilot would have to do.

Instructors also reminded each one of the former 'prop types' that they must place a particular emphasis on all of the items that were new to them within the F-86F, such as use of the radio compass, jet instrument techniques and cruise control.

Before any thought could be given to actually flying the F-86, the function of every instrument, and the procedures adopted when dealing with an emergency, had to be memorised, for a written exam based on both aspects of the jet was the next test for would-be Sabre pilots. This quiz 'covered all the bases' such as correct air start procedures, fuel quantities (with and without external tanks), fuel tank feeding sequence, tank capacities, mach limits and G limits for given gross weights and external loads, and maximum speeds for lowering gear and flaps. In addition to the written examination, the Instructor Pilot (IP) would give each pilot the blindfold cockpit check, followed by an intense oral quiz. By the time an individual was cleared to begin flying the F-86F, he had a thorough working knowledge of everything to hand inside his cockpit.

The actual training flights for both wings consisted of the following:

- familiarisation flights of the area (1 hour 40 minutes)
- basic instruments and IFR (Instrument Flight Rules) letdown (1 hour 30 minutes)
- basic instruments, GCA (Ground-Controlled Approach – radar), navigation and cruise control exercise (3 hours 50 minutes)
- aerobatics (50 minutes)
- introduction to formation flying, with two-ship and then four-ship (4 hours 30 minutes)
- night landings and tight four-ship formations (1 hour 30 minutes)
- four flights for air-to-air gunnery practice (each 50 minutes, and part of the advanced course)
- five flights in air-to-ground gunnery (each 50 minutes, and part of the advanced course)

With the basic training syllabus and the first two steps in the advanced course completed, the final 'step' in the

work-up saw the pilot undertake two fighter sweeps over the Yalu with the CCTF instructors. Having passed all of these tests successfully, the pilot was now considered combat ready.

A minimum of three T-33 two-seat jet trainers were required at Osan in order to handle the sheer volume of conversion work. These were duly borrowed from nearby F-84 squadrons, and by the end of February 1953, the 18th FBW had 76 pilots checked out in the new fighter. Of these, only eight per cent were combat ready, however, with a further 28 per cent in the final stages of training. The remaining 64 per cent of the pilots still had a long way to go before taking Sabres up north – as did the the 18th FBW.

To make matters worse for the FEAF, the first squadron within the 8th FBW had also just stood down, effectively making the Fifth Air Force four fighter-bomber squadrons light in Korea.

In order to speed up the conversion, part of the original plan put forward by the FEAF was for the 4th and 51st FIWs to loan two experienced F-86 pilots apiece to the 12th FBS. These Sabre veterans would lead the first MiG sweeps by the unit along the Yalu, but 18th FBW records show that at no time were there more than three interceptor pilots available to the wing during the

LEFT *There is an old saying that goes 'when you lose your sense of humour, the next thing to go will be your mind!' Fortunately, Osan boasted more than its fair share of comic individuals in 1953. One such figure was Lt Harold Colladay, who is seen taking a peek out of his Sabre's intake for the benefit of the camera. Colladay was amongst the first group of pilots to transition onto the F-86F with the 67th FBS (Harold Colladay)*

transition period. Ironically, later that year (by which time all three squadrons within the 18th FBW were well and truly 'up and running') there were as many as eight experienced interceptor pilots working with the wing!

LAST SHOOTING STARS

As mentioned in the first chapter, the 80th FBS had the honour of being the last squadron to utilise the F-80 in combat. The Shooting Star had been the first jet fighter to see action in Korea, and it had performed well. In the early days, F-80s were used in the fighter interceptor role, and they had been retained in this mission until the first F-86As arrived in-theatre in December 1950.

The 80th FBS was also the last of the six Sabre fighter-bomber squadrons to convert over to the F-86F. Although they were not able to stand down until 1 May 1953, within two weeks they were operational with the new jet, even though they did not receive their full complement of aircraft until 4 June. The reason for this delay was that the unit's jets arrived with ultra-high frequency radio sets fitted by mistake. It took almost a month to replace these with useable equipment, so in the meantime, the 80th FBS continued to set records in their older F-80Cs.

Lt Robert D Rawlings was a 'Head Hunter' during the transition period from the Shooting Star to the Sabre;

'As the last squadron to fly the F-80 in combat, it was a great lift to have brand new F-86Fs delivered to us as

replacements. The F-80s were so beat-up from almost three years in the frontline that they were really hazardous to fly. One of them even had reverse controls! I'll never forget when the new Sabres arrived at Suwon, with only about ten hours of time on each of them. We were like kids with new toys as we picked out the ones to be assigned to us! The vast difference in time over the target (F-80 versus F-86) was a tremendous safety factor to all of us. The enemy gunners had a lot of trouble leading us enough to score solid hits. It was definitely to our advantage to be in the F-86s.'

The significance of an active combat wing (18th FBW) converting from an out-dated aircraft to one that would be considered state-of-the-art – and doing so in a forward combat zone – has never really been fully appreciated. When detailing this episode as part of their examination of the air force's role in the Korean War, the USAF History Office states;

'We cannot find another example of such a drastic conversion in the history of the Air Forces. In World War 2, all of the fighter equipment changes were piston- to piston-engine. B-17/B-24 conversions to the new B-29 were all done in CONUS (Continental United States). The most drastic was the 1945 conversion of one squadron of twin-engined A-20s to four-engined B-32s in the Philippines. Nothing else in Korea or South-east Asia matches the F-51 to F-86 conversion done by the 18th Wing.'

BELOW *This wintery view of the ramp at Osan AB was taken during the latter stages of the 18th FBW's conversion. The yellow or red bands on the respective fins of these aircraft designated which squadron the Sabres were assigned to – red meant the 67th FBS and yellow the 12th FBS (F G Smart)*

Maj Flamm D Harper was Operations Officer for the 18th FBW, and he is seen here posing in his F-86F immediately prior to flying another combat mission from Osan AB. Maj Harper was responsible for planning the bold nocturnal strikes flown by the wing against two marshalling yards (each packed with around 100 boxcars carrying ammunition) situated close to the frontline. Although at least two Sabres were lost during the mission, the munitions trains were completely destroyed, and a massive Chinese offensive thwarted in the process (F D Harper)

WARNING
THIS AIRPLANE CONTAINS A SEAT
EJECTION CATAPULT CONTAINING

CHAPTER 3

NEW SABRES IN COMBAT

Virtually all the fighter-bomber pilots that transitioned onto the F-86F were lacking in the art of fighter interceptor tactics, having previously revelled in the tag of 'mud movers', or 'low-level metal magnets'. As such, their chosen profession did not 'score big' with the media, for it failed to have the swashbuckling glamour associated with the air-to-air dogfighters of the fighter interceptor squadrons. However, now that the F-86F had come into play, that was all about to change. From now on, they would be fighting in both arenas.

To the naked eye, there was very little to differentiate the fighter interceptor F-86F from the fighter-bomber F-86F. Indeed, the primary differences between the two types amounted to bomb shackles, a modification to the gun/bomb/rocket sight and special external fuel tanks, all of which were fitted to the FBW variant.

At first, there were many sceptics that said the Sabre would not work in the 'mud mover' role – it was much too fast, and it would probably be unstable with heavy bomb loads. These 'myths' were soon dispelled, however, by men such as 18th FBG Operations Officer, Capt Flamm D Harper, who was one of the experienced interceptor types brought in to help mould the new wing into a first class F-86 outfit. Not long after both he and Capt Ebersole had arrived at K-55, they received spot promotions to major. Harper remembers;

'The Sabre was an excellent "mud-mover", for it could carry two 1000-lb bombs, two external fuel tanks and 1800 rounds of 0.50-cal to any target in North Korea. Due to its speed, the jet took us far less time to accomplish the missions. We could also carry napalm, but we were never tasked to do so. We did some skip bombing, and speed did not prove to be a problem at all.'

As each pilot in both wings reached the final stages of their conversion to the F-86, the anticipation of their first combat missions in the new aircraft really excited them.

They would first have to complete several fighter sweeps over 'MiG Alley' before they were allowed to return to bomb dropping, however. Each of these missions would be led by experienced interceptor pilots.

USAF records show that from January through to June 1953, the 18th FBW was credited with seven MiG-15s destroyed, three probables and ten damaged, without a single loss to enemy aircraft. However, during this same period, the wing lost ten Sabres to ground fire – delivering ordnance at low level over heavily defended targets was still extremely dangerous, just as it had been during the (appreciably slower) Mustang era.

One of the most experienced pilots to fly with the 18th FBW was 67th FBS commander, Maj James Hagerstrom, who was not only a truly gifted exponent of fighter-bomber tactics, but also a World War 2 fighter ace – he had scored six kills flying P-40 Warhawks with the 8th FS/49th FG in the South Pacific in 1943/44. Hagerstrom made no bones about his desire to shoot down MiGs, and that is exactly what he did best. He had originally joined the 4th FIW in September 1952, and subsequently destroyed two MiG-15s, claimed a third as a probable and damaged three more by year-end flying E- and F-models with the 334th and 335th FISs.

Hagerstrom then became one of the original 4th FIW pilots transferred to the 18th FBW in January 1953, being given command of the 67th FBS. Thanks to his efforts, and those of the other instructor pilots assigned to the wing, by the last week of February there were enough suitably qualified pilots within the 18th FBW to fly a few fighter sweeps over 'MiG Alley'. On the 25th, Maj Hagerstrom led the first such combat mission.

It had been decided by the instructors prior to the conversion actually even starting that the first 'order of business' for the new pilots after completing the 'check out' phase was for them to become familiar with the interceptor mission. To this end, the first combat sorties flown by all three squadrons within the 18th FBW were against MiG-15s over the Yalu.

Returning to the 25 February mission, Maj Hagerstrom fittingly claimed the wing's first kill with the F-86F when he shot down a MiG-15 near Konha-dong. Just over a month later, on 27 March, the major was again leading a flight of 18th FBW Sabres through 'MiG Alley' when they jumped a number of MiG-15s, and Hagerstrom 'bagged' two in five minutes. This took the veteran pilot's tally to 6.5 MiG victories (he had claimed 1.5 kills exactly two weeks earlier), and made him the 28th USAF ace of the Korean War (see *Osprey Aircraft of the Aces 4 - Korean War Aces* for further details). He finished his tour with 8.5 kills, 1 probable and 5 damaged, with all of these claims being made against MiG-15s.

ABOVE *From the time the 8th FBW became operational with the F-86F, most, if not all, of its aircraft carried names on their respective noses, rather than the elaborate artwork synonymous with other Korean Sabre wings. Boasting distinctive red sun burst tail markings, these jets belong to the 36th FBS, which was the first unit in the wing to covert from the F-80 to the F-86F. This impressive flightline shot was taken at Suwon AB (K-13) in June 1953 (Dick Seger)*

8th FBW

Whilst the 18th FBW was enjoying its new fighter role at Osan, over at Suwon AB (K-13), the 8th FBW was also nearing the end of its conversion onto the F-86F. By 7 April the 36th FBS 'Flying Fiends' were considered sufficiently advanced enough to fly their first MiG sweep, although this proved to be uneventful. Six days later, the squadron got down to the business at hand – bombing. The very next day the 18th FBW also conducted its first bombing sorties.

The F-86F-30 had already started to make a name for itself over the battlefields of Korea, and its most impressive missions were yet to come.

During the spring both wings perfected their close support/interdiction tactics, and some of the initial reports that were published following these early sorties stated that the F-86F had excellent stability on the bomb runs, and that this characteristic was essential for bombing accuracy. The Sabre also had a low vulnerability to ground fire, which was enhanced by its great speed.

Among the pilots that were taking the new fighter-bomber into MiG-infested areas, there was absolutely no fear of being jumped, for they were confident that they would prevail with the F-86F. In other words, the versatility of the Sabre was limited only by the capabilities of the pilot that was flying it. Although these reports spoke primarily about the aircraft as a bomber, they also placed a heavy emphasis on the fighter interceptor (FI) role, stating that this phase of the wing's mission should be participated in regularly by pilots from both the 8th and 18th FBWs. This would avoid either wing losing proficiency in this area, for the lose of the interceptor mission effectively negated the reason for having the Sabre in the frontline as a multi-role fighter.

As the two wings worked up to full combat strength, small problems and 'glitches' cropped up, although most of these could be corrected with little 'fanfare'. One such technical 'hiccup' involved the external drop tanks. Whenever the Sabres would begin to line up for their bombing targets, or if they had sighted MiGs, they would 'punch off' the tanks. However, after the first combat mission it was found that the departing tanks inflicted extensive damage on the outer wing panels and pitot masts. Newly-promoted Maj Howard Ebersole commented on these problems;

ABOVE LEFT *A flight of three 35th FBS Sabres return from a bombing mission over North Korea in June 1953. The sleek jets pulled in close to give Lt Joe Lynch a chance to shoot some good aerial photography, with* Lt Herbert Schimsk's Dixie Belle *positioning just off Lynch's right wing. In the final weeks of conflict before the ceasefire was brokered, the 8th FBW was sending up 16- and 24-ship gaggles (each aircraft being armed with 1000-lb bombs) to attack the bridges at Sinanju. This target was probably the most heavily defended in all of Korea, and many F-86s and F-84s were shot full of holes while on their bombing runs (Joseph Lynch)*

BELOW LEFT *A good, clean, side view of a 35th FBS Sabre parked at Suwon AB in the summer of 1953. The jet's assigned pilot was* Lt James Firebaugh, who had named it Kitty and Martain's Cotton Picker *after his wife and daughter. Most of the missions flown by Firebaugh over North Korea were against road cuts and bridges. He eventually ended up performing a second combat tour in Vietnam flying C-123Ks with the 606th Special Operations Squadron (James Firebaugh)*

Lt Frank Harrison's Sabre sits idle on the ramp at Osan (K-55) in July 1953. During the final three months of the war, the 18th FBW burnt up close to 1,000,000 gallons of jet fuel each month, with the wing's Sabres averaging 52 hours of use per month in June – this figure increased in July. As a tribute to the maintenance crews, the percentage of aircraft in service for June and July was slightly higher than the 92 per cent figure achieved in the spring. This allowed the wings to drop more than 2400 bombs apiece in each month (Frank Harrison)

'The tanks did damage to the wings, and they were also very expensive to simply lose after a single sortie. When we punched a pair off, we would say "there goes another Cadillac"! I think it cost the air force something like $5000 for each set. Instead of dropping straight down, they would fly up and knock off the pitot tube. This could create a potentially serious problem when you approached the base to land, for you had no idea what your airspeed was. Fortunately, none of our guys had any close calls because of this.'

With all four Sabre wings (4th and 51st FIWs and the 8th and 18th FBWs) now up and running at full strength, a far greater problem quickly arose – the maintenance departments for each wing were not equipped for the heavy workload of servicing and repairs generated by the intense cycle of frontline sorties now being flown. To make matter worse, the two interceptor wings were operating a mix of E- and F-models, although the fighter-bomber wings were equipped exclusively with brand new F-86F-30 models.

Back at Tsuiki AB, in Japan, the Rear Echelon Maintenance Combined Operations (REMCO) had been formed prior to the final Sabre wing conversions.

REMCO's brief was to help alleviate the servicing burden in the frontline, and as such, it would prove to be instrumental in allowing all four wings to boast high 'in service' rates through to the end of the war. Most field maintenance and, with few exceptions, all major inspections were performed at REMCO.

The first F-86F-30 sent back to Tsuiki for major work came from the 12th FBS as early as 29 March 1953. During the March/April period, the average turnaround time for work performed on a high-time Sabre was 7.34 days – the total time for any one fighter to be out of combat averaged out at about seven days. In April alone, 26 F-86s passed through REMCO, before being returned to their forward bases.

INCREASED AAA THREAT

During the autumn of 1952, the Chinese had increased the number of Anti-Aircraft Artillery (AAA) batteries deployed around strategic targets both in the north and further south. Indeed, the progress that the communists had made in this area in just one year was astounding.

During the first two years of the war, most of the heavy AAA had been located around key targets in the

ABOVE LEFT PRETTY PATTI *was assigned to the 67th FBS and flown by Lt Robert Doyle. FEAF senior commanders felt that the most difficult phase of the transition training for 18th FBW pilots would come when they attempted to embrace the fighter interceptor role. Needless to say, the fighter-bomber pilots took to the air-to-air mission like a duck to water, with the thought of killing a MiG-15 being the ultimate motivator! (Robert Doyle)*

BELOW LEFT *Maj Howard Ebersole, Operations Officer for the 12th FBS, sits in the cockpit of his Sabre at K-55. He was one of the most experienced leaders in the wing, and had flown numerous missions in fighter interceptor Sabres before joining the 18th. He and Maj James Hagerstrom were the first instructor pilots assigned to the wing when it began receiving its new F-models. This was the major's second 'shooting war', for he had flown B-24s during World War 2 (Howard Heiner)*

ABOVE *This view of an F-86F instrument panel was taken by Lt Kenneth Smith during a 'down day' for his unit. More than half of the sorties flown by the 12th FBS during the May-June period saw the squadron performing close support missions either over, or in the immediate vicinity of, the frontline. Such sorties required the direction of experienced FACs, for the frontline was continually shifting during this period due to the constant pressure applied on UN troops by communist forces probing for weaknesses (Ken Smith)*

north of Korea. This meant that the slower F-51 Mustangs had not been fully exposed to this concentrated, accurate ground fire. However, both the F-80s and F-84s had felt the full force of this barrage, and although the Thunderjets were able to absorb tremendous amounts of punishment and still get back home, the Shooting Stars were suffering mortal blows.

When dealing with manually-sighted AAA batteries, 'speed was life', and the F-86Fs could drop their bombs and exit the area at close on to 700 mph, whereas the F-80C could barely better 600 mph in level flight. However, by April 1953 the communists had been able to move their deadly AAA down into frontline areas to protect their troops and supply caches. This meant that even with its speed advantage over previous frontline jet types, the Sabre fighter-bombers were now also suffering mounting losses to the withering ground fire that surrounded virtually every target they attacked.

A good example of what the pilots had to face is revealed in the following account by Maj Howard Ebersole, who led a flight of 12th FBS jets on an interdiction mission north of the 'bomb line' on 10 June 1953. FEAF Intelligence had pin-pointed a large supply dump that it believed was feeding the needs of a substantial number of enemy troops. The 18th FBW was tasked with 'taking it out';

'I was leading "D" Flight, with Capt Bob Coury leading one of the elements. On my wing was Lt Sam Shattuck, and on Coury's wing was Lt Rick Westcott. On paper, it appeared to be a routine mission, but it proved to be anything but that! I found the target, lined it up with the sun at my back and rolled over into a 45-degree dive. I put the manual pipper on the target, and at about 3000 ft I "pickled off" two 1000-lb bombs. At the time, I didn't recall seeing any flak. Then the other three in the flight – Shattuck, Coury and Westcott – dropped their bombs.

'As Shattuck pulled up, his bombs set off some huge secondary explosions. As Coury went in, one of the guys called out to watch the flak, as it was getting close. There was no doubt that we had stirred up a Hornet's nest!

'At about that time, Coury got on the radio and indicated he had been hit. As I glanced over to check him out, I noticed that he was streaming a 100-ft torch of flame out of his tailpipe! I told him to try and make it back over friendly territory by steering one-eight-zero. He just cleared "Old Papa-San" mountain (which was held by the enemy), and as he made it over the other side he punched out. His F-86F (52-4339) exploded as soon as he ejected. He parachuted safely to the ground.

'As I dropped down to check out the burning wreckage, I noticed a huge man emerge from a cave and climb onto a "quad-fifty" AAA emplacement. My nose was pointed squarely at him, and as I squeezed the trigger, my 0.50-cal rounds converged right into him. The gun emplacement and gunner exploded right in front of my eyes! Bob Coury was captured and repatriated at the end of the war. We lost a lot of aircraft and several good pilots on these types of missions.'

The 8th FBW also suffered its share of losses to ground fire, as 35th FBS pilot Lt Herbert Schimsk recalls;

'The first combat mission I remember was a 16-ship formation that was sent to hit the well-defended bridges at Sinanju. I was the No 4 man in the fourth flight. We reached the target on time, and immediately launched our attack. As we rolled in on the bridges, I noted that one of our aircraft in the preceding flight had been hit.

'It appeared to me that the anti-aircraft fire had shot off his right wing, causing the Sabre to spin uncontrollably. The pilot did not eject. We continued our runs, and after I dropped my "thousand pounders", I noted the AAA guns just off either end of the bridges, but it was too late for me to bring my 0.50-cal guns in line with them. Speed, angle and altitude would not allow it. A return pass was out of the question, as duelling with 37 mm guns with 0.50-cals was not conducive to surviving the war! After returning from the mission, I learned that the pilot of the Sabre that went in was a good friend of mine. It was a tough way to break into the bomber business.'

Another tragedy struck the 8th FBW in June, although the loss was not caused by heavy AAA fire,

BELOW PEGGY ANN *was 'owned' by crew chief S/Sgt George Banasky. In an unwritten understanding dating back to World War 2, it was common knowledge amongst pilots and crew chiefs that the aircraft 'belonged' to the latter individual, and it was only 'borrowed' by the pilot for short periods of time! Banasky had earlier crewed a 12th FBS F-51D during the fighter's final days with the unit. Most aircraft that served in the Korean War featured the name of their crew chief stencilled on the right side of the forward fuselage, along with a nickname or nose-art of his choosing (George Banasky)*

ABOVE *Crew Chief Sgt Vic Collier kneels down beside one of the 1000-lb bombs that has been recently shackled onto 'his' 67th FBS F-86F. The primary load for the Sabre fighter-bomber was either a pair of 500- or 1000-lb GP bombs. HVAR rockets were rarely used, and napalm was employed on just a handful of missions during the early days of the F-model's operational service with the 8th and 18th FBWs. In the last three months of the war, the larger 'thousand pounder' became the favoured ordnance 'of choice'* (Vic Collier)

rather a random hit from a lucky enemy soldier. 1Lt Robert McDermott, who was a pilot in the 80th FBS, recalls being part of a four-ship mission that was hunting for road traffic on an early-morning mission;

'We took off a first light from Suwon. As we moved into our patrol area north of the frontlines, we split up into elements and started looking for anything that was moving on the roads. My wingman was 2Lt Joseph Quagley, and our ordnance load consisted of two 1000-lb GP bombs each. Suddenly, Joe called out that he had seen some trucks below and was going down to check them out. Seconds later, I saw this ball of fire streaming down toward the ground. I called out on the radio, but there was no answer. I recall that there was no ground fire or shooting that I was aware of.

'I immediately called in that one of our aircraft was down, and I wasn't sure of my exact position. Control told me to gain some altitude and they would get a fix on my

position, which I did. After giving them all the info I could, I circled the area and went down low again. I lined up on a road target and dropped by bombs. During this run, I did not draw any fire from the ground. Lt Quagley had made his low-level pass directly across the road and not parallel. 'The only thing I can surmise is that small arms fire got a lucky hit on his fuel tank. There was no explosion, so his ordnance had not been dropped. I kept hoping that his name would appear on the PoW list at the end of the war, but it never did.'

INTERCEPTOR MISSIONS

The 35th and 36th FBSs spent a lot of their early operational time in the Sabre flying the interceptor mission because a significant number of their aircraft were not yet fitted with bomb racks. Despite this, the 8th FBW failed to score a single confirmed jet kill with the Sabre, even though they flew hundreds of hours over 'MiG Alley'

LEFT *'Pulling' alert duty during the Korean summers was not the most sought after job. Here, Lt Marvin Patton (a pilot in the 35th FBS) uses his locally-purchased umbrella to ward off the sun. Aside from the wings of his jet, the parasol provided the only shade to be found out on the flightline at Suwon. Each of the three squadrons within the 8th FBW was tasked with providing a certain number of aeroplanes and pilots for alert duty, and this remained an ongoing tasking long after the war had ended (Marvin Patton)*

Each Sabre had at least two groundcrewmen assigned to keep it in full working order, and Sgt Vic Collier (on the right) was part of the team that serviced FU-371. Like all 67th FBS aircraft (including the unit's T-33), this Sabre proudly wears the squadron's distinctive boxing rooster emblem just aft of its gun troughs. Unusually, in this instance the cockerel has been painted on the starboard rather than the port side. ''MOVIN' ON'' was photographed soon after returning from a mission, its groundcrew taking a break from the early stages of the aircraft's pre-sortie turn-around (Vic Collier)

during the early summer of 1953. Lt Herbert Schimsk remembers his early days with the 35th FBS;

'My first flight assignment in the squadron was to serve as the CO's wingman on combat air patrols over North Korea. We were strictly looking for MiGs. The squadron's Operations Officer made it very clear to me that my only objective on this mission was to fly wing and stay with the CO, no matter what!! I stuck to him like glue, and apparently I did OK because I was scheduled with him on several future missions. The flights up to the river were long and boring, since we never encountered enemy aircraft. Once we received our bomb racks, I was able to fly with my flight. Later on, we found out that the 4th and 51st FIWs were always given the patrols that had any chance of meeting the MiGs!

'On the first pre-planned mission that the 8th FBW flew after receiving our bomb racks, we scheduled 24 Sabres. There would be 12 F-86Es from the 51st FIW flying top cover for us. The 8th took off with only 23 Sabres due to a maintenance problem. However, five minutes after everyone took off, the lone F-86F we had left behind launched with two 1000-lb GP bombs under his wings. He rapidly closed the gap and soon joined up with our escorts from the 51st. Once the pilot noted their chequered tails, he moved on forward to find our 8th FBW aircraft, and complete his mission.

'This episode demonstrated the advantage of the "F" over the "E". The 51st FIW was never able to catch the 8th FBW to provide top cover since they flew older model Sabres boasting only 5200 lbs st of thrust – our Sabres had 6090 lbs st thrust engines. From that time on, it was determined that we did not need top cover to protect us from the MiG-15s.'

By the final two months of the war, the Sabre fighter-bomber pilots had become very proficient at their work. And If there was an inexperienced pilot flying within a typical flight of four, it was compensated for by the wealth of experience provided by the flight and element leaders.

For the deep penetration missions into northern Korea, weather was not a factor because there were no friendly troops in close proximity to the targets that they were tasked with hitting. Lt James Setterberg of the 35th FBS flew

ABOVE LEFT *Lt. John Crocker broils in the shade of an umbrella whilst carrying out alert duty at Osan in the late summer of 1953. If the alarm had sounded, his F-86F would have been airborne in a matter of minutes. The take-off roll on the Sabre was a little over 3000 ft, whilst its average airspeed during the closing stages of an interception was usually about 520 mph (422 knots) (Frank Harrison).*

BELOW LEFT *The crew chief for FU-336 poses in his winter jacket during the early spring of 1953 – this particular 67th FBS Sabre was assigned to Lt Cliff Nunnery. The interior detail of the starboard mid-fuselage-mounted airbrake is well exposed in this photograph. In a heated aerial battle, these devices were important in keeping the pursuing Sabre from overshooting his intended victim. If they malfunction-ed, the hunter could become the hunted in just a matter of seconds (Cliff Nunnery)*

ABOVE Having been off-loaded from the bomb truck, these 'thousand pounders' will eventually be up-lifted onto FU-389. The 1000-lb GP bomb proved to be devastatingly effective against bridges and powerplants in the extreme northern sectors of North Korea. Such targets became the 'staple diet' for F-86F crews, for by the time this photograph was taken in the spring of 1953, there were no moving targets to be found during daylight hours (Cliff Nunnery)

a number of these missions, and here he elaborates on how dangerous they could be in bad weather;

'Of the 47 missions that I flew in the F-86F before the war ended, the toughest were those called MPQs. These were radar-controlled missions, where we flew in groups of three aircraft. We would take off from Suwon AB with the flight leader in the middle and a single Sabre on either side of him. The ceilings were always very low on these sorties, and we would enter cloud at an altitude of about 500 ft. On many missions, it was so thick that my leader's wing tip was only about 18 inches away from my canopy. I literally could not make out his fuselage!

'On one of the interdiction missions, I was flying on the wing of the CO of the 8th FBW. There were 48 Sabres that launched together. Everyone was jammed on the runway, and we all "gave it power" at the same time. I was the second element in line, so the jet wash wasn't

bad, but further back in the chain it was very rough! Each F-86 carried two 500-lb bombs, and our target was the airfield at Sinuiju, which was right up on the Yalu.

'Often, our recce aircraft would spot MiGs parked there, but as soon as the communists knew we were coming, they would fly over to Antung, on the Manchurian side of the border.

'En route, we were up at 36,000 ft, lining up for our bomb run. We had to level off at 26,000 ft, and when we reached this altitude, the sky turned black all around us. The enemy had been plotting our let-down. If it hadn't been for the undercast, a lot of us would have taken hits from the intense AAA fire. Col Benz immediately broke us up into elements so we could find holes in the cloud cover, get below it and finish our mission.

'As I was in a steep dive toward my target, I could see the AAA gunners on their rotating mounts. They had a

BELOW *2Lt Dick Iglehart of the 12th FBS pulls in close for the camera en route to Japan. All 8th and 18th FBW Sabres had to be ferried back to the Rear Echelon Maintenance facility (REMCO) in Japan for major maintenance work, and these overwater flights were usually performed in pairs. Having delivered their war-weary jets to the factory, the pilots would in turn fly back in Sabres that were ready for further frontline service. The average turn-around time for major maintenance was seven to nine days (Frank Harrison)*

BELOW *The port 0.50-cal Colt-Brownings of Lt John W Dawson's* NAUGHTY NELLY *undergo major maintenance. The presence of a tow bar attached to the jet's nose gear leg indicates that this photograph was probably taken whilst the Sabre was on the firing range, having its guns bore-sighted. Six machine guns was the standard fit for all versions of the F-86 used by the USAF in Korea, although a handful of 4th FIW jets were fitted with four 20 mm cannon and successfully trialled in aerial combat. They were not, however, used in the ground attack role (John Dawson)*

large number of these units defending the airfield. After releasing both of my bombs, I immediately went out over the river at little more than ten feet above the water. The guns on both sides were firing as low as they could go, and I was *below* their line of fire. They were literally firing at each other from both sides of the Yalu! I stayed low and flew right on out of the mouth of the river and over the Yellow Sea, before I started gaining altitude. The flight back to Suwon was uneventful.'

On many squadron or wing launches, there were often 24 or more Sabres lined up for take-off. Once en route to the target area, if a pilot found that there was even the smallest fault with his aircraft, standing FEAF orders dictated that he had to abort the mission and take his wingman back to base with him. There was no room for deviation on this point, even if the jet was being flown by a wing or squadron commander.

An example of this ruling being followed to the letter came during a major mission that was flown on 13 June 1953 by the 18th FBW. The wing put up six four-ship

flights, the first three of which were from the 12th FBS and the fourth from the 67th. The gaggle was led by 12th FBS CO, Lt Col Harry Evans.

Approaching an area often patrolled by MiGs, the F-86F of Lt Col Evans developed a problem and he had to abort. At the same time, Lt William Barber had a hung drop tank, and both pilots, and their respective wingmen, departed the area and headed back to Osan. Capt Howard Mann took the lead, whilst his wing position was filled by Lt Don Forbes. Not long into the sweep, they spotted a flight of three MiGs ahead and below them.

One was far out in front of the other two, and Capt Mann dropped the nose of his jet and closed on this 'bogey' from the six o'clock position. At about 2000 ft astern off his foe, he fired several bursts but observed no hits. Closing to 1600 ft, Mann let fly a long burst and spotted multiple hits on the MiG's wing and fuselage. Seconds later, a small explosion was seen in the aft section of the fuselage, and the communist fighter started to trail a plume of black smoke. In the meantime, the two

remaining MiGs had closed the gap on the combatants, and Lt Forbes called out for his leader to 'break'.

Seeing both Sabres move into position to engage them, the two MiG-15 pilots broke off their attack and headed north over the river. At that time both 12th FBS F-86s resumed their patrol. Minutes later, two more MiG-15s engaged the element from below, and Mann turned into them. The subsequent dogfight developed into a series of 'scissors' manoeuvres in which the wingman in the MiG element spun out. Lt Forbes was then able to position himself behind the remaining MiG, and he duly fired a long burst from his six 0.50-cals. Numerous hits were noted, causing the enemy pilot to panic and snap roll his aircraft to the right. After three revolutions, the pilot ejected. With Capt Mann's earlier kill also being eventually confirmed, the element had bagged two MiGs for the 12th's record books.

'HUNTING'

Any pilot that ever flew an F-86 over North Korea auto-matically had the urge to 'sneak' across the border into Manchuria to do a little 'hunting' – this, of course, was strictly forbidden by the rules of engagement in place in Korea. Indeed, if all of the 'kills' that were made north of the Yalu River were officially recorded, the Sabre-versus-MiG kill ratio would have been significantly higher than it already was.

One of those pilots who flaunted the rules north of the Yalu was Lt Jack Magee. He had flown 90 missions in the F-80C while assigned to the 36th FBS, and when the time had come for his unit to convert onto the F-86, Magee was given the chance to stay on. He immediately signed up for at least 25 more sorties north.

Magee vividly recalls the days when ranking Korean ace Joe McConnell (of the 39th FIS) and veteran fighter pilot Howard Leaf (of the 25th FIS) came over to give the men of the 8th FBW some tips on air-to-air tactics. He also remembers some of the patrols that he flew up through 'MiG Alley', despite his primary mission being that of a fighter-bomber;

The 18th FBW suffered its fair share of operational losses with the F-86 during the final months of the war, as this photo clearly attests to! Numerous aircraft returned with serious battle damage, whilst others were written-off in non-combat related take-off and landing accidents. Once stripped of all useable spare parts, the gutted hulks were hauled to the Osan 'bone yard' – this view shows the 'Sabre cemetary' in the late summer of 1953. The yellow-nosed jets were from the 12th FBS and the all-silver F-86Fs from No 2 Sqn, SAAF (Reid Ivins)

RIGHT When not airborne, seeking out communist targets, Sabre pilots maintained their predatory skills by hunting for pheasant. The weapon of choice when going after game was a good, dependable, shotgun. The countryside around Osan was well stocked with wild fowl, and pilots became quite proficient at 'bagging' their fair share of birds — when the pheasants were out of season, the men turned to skeet shooting instead. Here, Lt Robert Niklaus proudly shows off his 'catch of the day'. Hunting was one of the few recreational activities enjoyed by wing personnel at Osan that was not conducted on-base (Robert Niklaus)

'Our MiG sweeps were less than fruitful. By early 1953 they had learned to stay north of the river . . . most of the time. We did, however, enjoy being able to climb out faster and higher than some of the fighter interceptor guys from the 4th and 51st FIWs (many of whom were flying older F-86Es). Our F-models had 6090 lbs st thrust, and could easily cruise at 44,000 to 46,000 ft at about 0.86 Mach.

'We saw "zilch" south of the Yalu! Our orders firmly stated that we were to stay on our side. A lot of pilots could not deal with this. We had flown many F-80 missions "up north" and not been able to effectively counter the MiG threat. Now flying an aircraft better than the communist jet, we had no choice but to sneak over the line – IFF (Identification Friend or Foe) off, and in radio silence – and go looking for MiGs. Some of our guys recorded damaged claims during these unauthorised engagements.

'On one patrol I was flying in the No 3 slot, with another flight commander flying as lead. Silently, he took his element on over the river. I kept my element on the south side. We would pace up and down the area until our fuel gauge indicated we had to head home. The flight lead that went over the line didn't have any luck that day, but a few days later he did the same thing, and this time one of the Sabres went down. Fortunately, the pilot was picked up, for he had gotten his stricken aircraft out over the sea before he ejected. But, we had lost a valuable aircraft, and Fifth Air Force had a fit!

'They immediately ordered us back to "bomb hauling" only, being tasked to knock out bridges, railroad track and troop concentrations. When my obligation was up, I got out of that routine. Of the 100+ missions I flew in the F-86, only seven of them were in the air-to-air arena. To mark the end of my extended tour, I was allowed to lead the group on my last mission.'

FINAL OFFENSIVE

By early May 1953, the Chinese realised that the war could end at any time, and Red Army commanders were duly ordered by their political masters in Peking (now Beijing) to gain as much ground as possible before any cease-fire agreement was signed. If the army had to suffer heavy casualties in order to accomplish this directive, then so be it.

Lt Robert K Cassatt was a pilot in the 67th FBS's 'Rye Flight' in the final months of the conflict, and he and his

BELOW *This photograph, taken soon after sunrise on a Saturday morning at Osan AB in the early summer of 1953, shows the alert pilot and his groundcrew being inspected by the base wing commander. During the war years, missions were flown throughout the week, regardless of what day it was. This routine became a little more relaxed following the ceasefire, although the military regimen observed during the conflict continued on just as if the squadrons were still at war. For example, newly-arrived replacement pilots still had to undertake a strict indoctrination period to ensure that they were combat-ready just in case hostilities flared up again (Kenneth Koon)*

ABOVE *Wearing the distinctive multi-coloured sunburst marking on its tail, the F-86F assigned to the boss of the 8th FBW chases its shadow over mud flats off the North Korean coast. The jet is devoid of drop tanks, meaning that its pilot has either jettisoned these prior to bombing a target, or the aircraft is simply on a brief test 'hop' following a maintenance period (John Thompson)*

colleagues were heavily involved in repelling the renewed communist push south. Here, he recalls a late-war mission that had a particularly fraught conclusion;

'The Chinese had found a weakness in one of our frontline positions, and were making a major effort to break through. Our flight was called in to work with a FAC, and our target was to be a suspected ammo dump that was helping support the Chinese offensive. When we arrived in the area, we had to orbit for awhile because some navy Skyraiders were working the same target. It took some time because the Navy guys carried a tremendous amount of ordnance on those aircraft. Our four Sabres were loaded with two 1000-lb bombs each.

'Finally, we got the green light and peeled off from about 20,000 ft at 15-20 second intervals. We dove down to about 2500 ft, released our loads, and pulled out to avoid getting too close to the ground fire. We were almost vertical with our speed brakes extended. At this late stage of the war, the Chinese had sighted some very dangerous AAA pieces around their frontline positions (both 75 mm and 90 mm), but I don't remember seeing anything unusual on that day.

'As we pulled out, we retracted our brakes and our speed increased rapidly. For some reason or another, one of our pilot's bombs failed to jettison. Our flight lead stated that we would have to follow him out over the Yellow Sea to release the bombs. So far, it was rather routine, so we headed back to Osan (K-55). To our surprise and consternation, a thick layer of fog had covered the airfield. With fuel running low, we diverted over to the marine base at Pyongtaek (K-6). When we arrived overhead, night was falling rapidly, and we could barely see the ground, with the exception of the runway lights. As we approached on initial for break, we each had about 200 lbs of fuel left, which under normal circumstances would have given us about two minutes' worth of flying time.

'We broke for landing and started on final approach. I don't remember the exact sequence, but one or two aircraft went around and I landed. In the process, I blew both tyres thinking that the runway was much shorter than it actually was – it was actually about 7000 ft long, but had a hump in the middle so one could not see the far end! My plane went off the runway, as did another Sabre, but finally we were all down! There was no damage to the aircraft, but my ego had been wounded.

'We were damn lucky to get down, for if we had not found an open field when we did, we would have all been forced to bail out. It was the hairiest experience I had while flying combat in Korea!'

One of the traits that sets a fighter pilot apart from all other types is the fact that he *is* a fighter pilot! The ultimate goal for any military aviator is to fight in aerial combat and win. That lust for the kill is always there, even if a pilot is forced into the fighter-bomber arena. This rational applied to the men of the 8th and 18th FBWs, who were willing to risk fuel starvation in order to get one fleeting shot at the elusive swept-wing MiG-15. One such individual was Maj Raymond C Lee, who served as Operations Officer for the 35th FBS at Suwon in the final hectic weeks of the Korean War;

'When I arrived, I felt the war could not last much longer, and I got into the flying end of it at a very fast pace. I flew 22 missions during the last 23 days of the war. They included every type of mission – I destroyed a tank, got several secondary explosions from enemy ammuni-tion caches, bombed the big bridge over the Yalu and, with my squadron commander, Lt Col Robert Scott, looked for MiGs over the Yalu.

Sightings were rare, however, because communist pilots also evidently sensed that the war was coming to an end, and they were very careful not to fly over the Yellow Sea or south of Sinanju.

'Our procedure was to select a target as far into North Korea as possible, place our ordnance on it, and then immediately climb toward "MiG Alley". Our search for MiGs had to be short because of fuel limitations. We were very careful to turn off our IFF boxes before proceeding. We chased a few jets, but couldn't catch them.

'Lt Col Scott was a superb pilot, who really knew how to fly the F-86 to the edge of its limits. On the way home, we "stopcocked" at 35,000 ft and rode the "Siberian wind" to Seoul, re-started in the glide down and landed at K-13 with minimum fuel. This was definitely a VFR (Visual Flying Rules) only operation!'

BELOW *By the spring of 1953, the new 'super base' at Osan had begun to take shape. The supporting squadrons within the wing had their own buildings, and the roads that criss-crossed the base were built up to prevent them turning into mud pits following rain. Conversely, during the dry summer months the roads were oiled to reduce the levels of dust stirred up by truck traffic. This shot shows both an oiled road and the 18th Supply Squadron's facilities, whilst the 'tent city' on the side of the hill in the background served as living quarters for a large number of wing personnel (John Batchelder)*

ABOVE An early-morning briefing at Osan calls for a major strike against North Korean targets, with heavy participation from No 2 Sqn, SAAF, whose pilots can be seen seated to the right of this photograph – to the left are personnel from both the 12th and 67th FBSs. As sortie rates rose, so the wing was forced to strike a balance between attacking major targets along the Yalu River and supporting friendly troops under fire in the frontline. The latter sorties were usually worked in around long-range penetration missions, for strikes deep into North Korea (invariably against fixed targets) were almost always pre-planned (Archie Buie)

LEFT *Minor maintenance and preparation for a mission continue against the backdrop of an approaching summer thunderstorm. In the spring months of both 1953 and 1954, Osan AB was subjected to drenching rains that flooded large areas of the base. However, by mid-1954 sufficient improvements had been made to the facility to allow it to cope with heavy rain, and any damage caused was quickly repaired (Robert Niklaus)*

MAIN PICTURE *Subjected to extremes of temperature, Sabre groundcrews battled mud and rain in the spring, dust and oppressive heat in the summer, and frequent snow storms in the winter. This photograph shows the aftermath of a snow squall that passed through Osan during the winter of 1953/54. Even though the war had concluded seven months earlier, the wing conducted 'business as usual', regardless of the inclement weather. Note that snowploughs have had to clear the taxyway to the main runway. Parked in the distance (to the right of the Sabres) are two USAF C-47s, which performed daily shuttle flights between Japan and Osan, carrying supplies and spare parts, as well as base personnel travelling back and forth on R&R. Osan's tower can also be seen behind the red-nose 67th FBS F-86F (Kenneth Koon)*

INSET *With aircraft covered in several inches of snow from an overnight fall, Operations personnel from wing HQ have employed a Jeep to travel out to the ramp to check whether aircraft scheduled for the morning's missions will be ready for their pre-arranged take-off slots. Clearly, the 67th FBS Sabre in the background is not on the roster for the first 'push'! While bases in South Korea received their fair share of snow and ice, it was the weeks of freezing temperatures that took a toll on men and equipment (William Barber)*

FAR LEFT *Lt. Sam Harris, patrolling at altitude, snaps a self-portrait through his rear view mirror. Harris was a pilot with the 35th FBS, and he flew most of his tour during the immediate postwar period, when long flights along the Korean coast were the order of the day. Although the 8th FBW finally moved back to its old prewar base at Itazuke, Japan, on 20 October 1954, the wing retained a presence in Korea through the regular deployment of flights of Sabres to Kunsan AB (Sam Harris)*

TOP LEFT *Devoid of underwing stores, Just Joan of No 2 Sqn slowly taxies back to its parking area at Osan at the end of yet another strike mission. The South Africans took part in the massive May Day raid against the radio station at Pyongyang, which proved to be one of the biggest missions of the war in terms of the total number of F-86s involved. Both the 4th and 51st FIWs provided top cover, whilst the 8th and 18th FBWs pounded the target (Reid Ivins)*

BOTTOM LEFT *The South African rugby team, comprised of No 2 Sqn personnel, was a crack side. During the unit's transition onto the Sabre, they took a couple of days off for a big match with the New Zealand forces team in Seoul. On 28 March 1953 a follow-up fixture was played against the Kiwis at Osan, and several matches were also staged against various British units – indeed, one of their toughest games involved a British Field Maintenance Unit. All matches were played on a professional level, even though there was a war going on. This team photo was snapped in July 1953 (Robert Niklaus)*

RIGHT *A pair of South African Sabres taxy past the parking area for the 67th FBS at Osan during the first few weeks of No 2 Sqn's transition period. Note that the USAF aircraft in the background are still wearing the original tail marking chosen for the 18th FBW, whilst the South African jets have the tri-chevron design (in their air force's national colours) that was later adopted wing-wide. No 2 Sqn began its transition onto the F-86F on 7 January 1953, initially flying dual-control T-33 until its pilots were considered ready to solo in the Sabre. Unit CO Ralph Gerneke and deputy commander Stan Wells were the first to solo on 30 January. Once all the pilots had flown solo on the Sabre, the squadron's first 'order of business' was to master fighter-interceptor tactics (Dick Kempthorne)*

TOP RIGHT *The maintenance work carried out by the 18th FBW's groundcrew proved to be a truly UN effort, for whenever a problem was encountered, personnel from all three squadrons would invariably get to work on fixing the 'broken' aircraft. For example, in this June 1953 photograph South African crewmen are being assisted by their counterparts from the 67th FBS. At this late stage in the war, the in-service rate for the F-86F was peaking in response to the heavy demand for the aircraft, and its bomb load (John Batchelder)*

BOTTOM RIGHT *This No 2 Sqn Sabre was photographed in the unfamiliar surroundings of Suwon AB during the final days of the war. The exact reason for its presence at the base is unrecorded, and one can only surmise that it had either been damaged in action and had had to effect an emergency landing, or it was participating in a joint mission with the resident 8th FBW. Parked behind the South African jet is a checkerboard-marked 39th FIS/51st FIW Sabre, this high-scoring fighter-interceptor wing also being based at Suwon (Archie Shaw)*

FAR RIGHT *The availability of replacement F-86Fs was at its highest right after the war had ended, for FEAF HQ made it a top priority to get all the fighter-bomber squadrons back up to full strength – both FBWs had received rough treatment from AAA batteries during the June-July period. Devoid of unit markings, one such replacement is seen here (at left) on the 67th FBW ramp (Robert Niklaus)*

CHAPTER 4

FACTS, FIGURES AND MORE WAR STORIES

BELOW *Having overseen the loading of two 1000-lb bombs on Lt John Field's F-86F by the ordnance crew, the crew chief for FU-364 conducts his final checks on the 0.50-cal magazines whilst the pilot finishes off his briefing and rides out to the flightline by Jeep. This 80th FBS aircraft carries the same sunburst marking on its tail as was worn on the unit's trusty F-80Cs. This shot was taken in June 1953 – the month in which the combined efforts of all six F-86F fighter-bomber squadrons resulted in over 3000 tons of bombs being dropped (John Field)*

Even though many good men gave their lives for the cause of freedom in Korea, and millions of dollars in equipment and material was spent during 37 months of bitter fighting on land and in the air, the conflict was never considered to be a 'real' war in the truest sense of the word. There were too many 'safe areas' for the enemy to retreat to, and when this happens, the will to win becomes greatly diminished. As if to prove this true, the final two years of the conflict in Korea saw the frontlines remain pretty well stagnant.

If there were any 'bright spots' to come out of the conflict, they had to be that the Republic of South Korea was saved for democracy, and that the transition from a World War 2 military to the 'jet age' military was achieved

under combat conditions. As a result, the experience received by pilots new to the jet age was second to none.

In recent years, many facts have surfaced about the various nationalities that were flying the MiG-15s met by the UN pilots over the Yalu River. Foreign units rotated in and out of Manchuria, and as with the US military forces, the Soviet Bloc viewed Korea as the ultimate training ground. The Red Air Force MiG pilots proved to be a good match for their USAF counterparts for much of the war. Yet, during the final months of fighting, a large number of the MiG pilots encountered seemed to be inexperienced, and many simply 'punched out' when an F-86 locked onto their tail.

To the Sabre pilots, the aggressive and extremely

competent enemy pilots of 1950-52 were referred to as 'honchos'. By USAF standards, the communist training regimen was at the opposite end of the spectrum, for the arrival of new American aircraft types in-theatre meant a slow, methodical training process. For the communists, such a changeover meant the wholesale replacement of combat units by entirely new, inexperienced squadrons.

The levels of experience within a USAF unit was layered, with the 'high-timers' in the majority. In many cases, a pilot did not work himself up to flight lead until he had flown about 75 missions. This rule not only pertained to the interceptor pilots, but also to the fighter-bomber types as well. As in all wars fought over the centuries, the USAF had found once again that experience was the key to survival.

NO RUN-DOWN

Although the frontline in Korea had been relatively stable for almost two years come 1953, and both sides seemed grudgingly satisfied with the territory that they occupied, the last eight months of war saw the fighter-bomber groups busier than ever before. From February 1953 through to the signing of the truce on 27 July, the number of sorties flown in support of ground troops, or against enemy supply storage centres, had grown to an all-time high. The large number of F-84s in-theatre, and the new F-86Fs from the 8th and 18th FBWs, had kept the Chinese bottled up, without much hope of sustaining their abortive final offensive.

In order to achieve the impressive sortie rates of the final months of the war, the FEAF had placed a heavy emphasis on combat theatre readiness training. From March through to July, new fighter-bomber pilots were given closely supervised training for a minimum of 30 to 40 hours before they were considered to be combat ready.

This regimen accounted for a large slice of the combat flying time available from each aircraft, and published reports from both FBWs stated that as much as one-third of their 'air time' was allotted to training flights. An immediate result of this new policy was the improvement in bombing accuracy achieved by the pilots – combat losses were also reduced. Despite all this training, operational commitments never took a back seat within the wings, however, for combat was their primary reason for being in Korea.

BELOW Lt Bob McDermott holds his pose for the camera whilst climbing into the cockpit of his 80th FBS Sabre at Suwon during the final weeks of the war. The heavy June 'blitz' saw some 14 F-86Fs lost to AAA. By the end of July 1953, there were a total of 297 Sabres in-theatre, 132 of which were fighter-bombers (Bob McDermott)

The South Korean work force played a vital part in providing labour for numerous jobs that needed to be performed on all major air bases in-theatre – this worker has been trained to help the ordnance section, unloading bombs from trucks near aircraft in their revetments. The wing armourers would then come in and physically up-load the weapons onto the waiting jets. This photograph was taken on the 35th FBS's flightline at Suwon in mid-June 1953 during the mission 'surge' to counter invading Chinese ground forces (Robert Odle)

ABOVE RIGHT *Maj Alex Boychuck of the 8th FBW prepares to climb in his Sabre at Suwon. The colourful markings worn by this aircraft indicate that it was assigned to the wing's commanding officer. The 8th was regularly tasked with bombing the large Suiho powerplant, located on the Yalu River close to Manchuria. This was one of the most dangerous targets assigned to the Sabre fighter-bombers due to the proliferation of AAA sites that surrounded it, and a large number of jets came home with flak holes in the wings and fuselage, although only a few were actually shot down (Lloyd Irish)*

BELOW RIGHT *It took a minimum of three well-trained maintenance types to keep each F-86 in service during the sortie 'surges' of June and July 1953. Prior to this, in May the number of interdiction missions flown by the 18th FBW peaked at 487, this figure dropping in the next two months as the emphasis shifted to immediate and pre-planned close support sorties – the latter two taskings accounted for over 1000 sorties in June alone. Crew Chief S/Sgt George Banasky, on the right, and two other supporting airmen show off 'their' PEGGY ANN, which was assigned to the 12th FBS at Osan (George Banasky)*

During the final three months of the war, still further restrictions and operational guidelines for Sabre fighter-bombers pilots came into effect. Now there were rules pertaining to the handling of every type of target, effectively banning 'freelance' search and destroy missions. These fundamental changes came about because several friendly positions were inadvertently hit by Sabre fighter-bombers. FEAF reacted by stating that every fighter-bomber pilot over the frontline had to be under the direct control of a FAC or tactical air co-ordinator before he was cleared to drop his ordnance. These procedures remain valid to this day for USAF close air support (CAS) aircraft.

Despite the additional restrictions, both FBWs continued to fly record numbers of sorties, and these have never been bettered by the USAF. Indeed, the records set by the 18th FBW in particular have remained intact for over 46 years. The peak month for interdiction type sorties was in May 1953, when the three squadrons within the wing flew a total of 487. This was a slight increase over April, which was the first month that the wing was considered able to muster up a 'maximum effort'. As targets diminished in June, so the sortie tally dropped to 314.

This decrease was not a sign that the FEAF was letting up on the enemy, however. The Chinese knew that the war was winding down fast, and efforts to re-supply their troops were increased accordingly. The problem for the Sabre wings was that the entire re-supply operation was carried out at night, which was the domain of the piston-engined B-26 Invader. They medium bombers enjoyed great success 'after dark', leaving very little for the F-86F pilots to bomb and strafe.

With few targets on offer to the FBWs behind the frontlines, attention turned to close support missions instead. Just how much emphasis was placed on the CAS role in the final months of the war can gauged by the following statistics for the 18th FBW. During the month of April 1953, the wing logged just 38 CAS sorties, but in May, the number jumped to 558, and in June, No 2 Sqn, combined with the 12th and 67th FBSs, launched 974 sorties in support of troops in the frontline.

The success of the two USAF aircraft types – the F-86F and F-84 – that were dominating the fighter-bomber mission, allied with the effective employment of the B-26 Invader night interdictor, meant that the Chinese were denied any chance of initiating an offensive against UN ground forces before the cease-fire. Many years after the war, facts began to emerge detailing just how massive

BELOW *Lone 12th FBS F-86F* BO HEMIAN BELLE II *has been 'put away for the night', shielded from the elements with a protective one-piece canvas intake and canopy covering. This aircraft had almost certainly flown a mission earlier in the day, and then been declared 'surplus to requirements' for the rest of the flying schedule. This photograph was taken at Osan in the summer of 1953, by which time there were more than 125 F-86Fs tasked with exclusively performing the fighter-bomber mission in-theatre (Sam Bourne)*

RIGHT *Like the 35th FBS, the 36th FBS 'Flying Fiends' could also trace their lineage back to World War 1, the unit having originally formed as the 36th Aero Squadron on 12 June 1917. Seeing extensive action across the South Pacific in World War 2, the 'Flying Fiends' were one of the first units selected to occupy Japan in the wake of VJ-Day. When the Korean War started five years later, the 36th FBS was still based in Japan, at Itazuke. As with the 35th FBS, the unit flew three different types of aircraft (F-51A, F-80C and F-86F) during the course of the Korean War (Paul Gushwa)*

the efforts made by Chinese logistics forces to reach the frontline were. Virtually all of these were foiled by UN forces, for the CAS and interdiction missions had been honed to a 'perfect science' by mid-1953.

FAST FIGHTER-BOMBER

One the F-86F's primary advantages over other Korean War-vintage aircraft was its high maximum speed (695 mph at 40,000 ft), and it was this factor which greatly appealed to fighter-bomber pilots in-theatre. It was no secret within the FEAF that the role of close air support was becoming more and more dangerous due to the proliferation of AAA sites scattered across the battlefield.

The 'Dash-30' Sabre could carry a heavy war load and still 'get in and out' fast. This effectively meant that the pilot strapped into his cockpit could minimise the level of his exposure to the AAA batteries – especially those deadly 37 mm guns.

Aside from its impressive turn of speed, the F-86F also boasted a unique gun/bombsight, which allowed pilots from both FBWs to achieve astounding accuracy with their 1000-lb bombs. One of those pilots was Capt Flamm Harper, 18th FBG Ops Officer;

'We could initiate a dive-bomb attack from practically any altitude. One excellent tactic against targets heavily

defended, or deep within enemy territory, was to approach from 30,000 ft or above, thus simulating fighter-interceptors on the enemy's radar. At 85 per cent power, and with speed brakes extended, we could dive towards the general area of the target at about a 50-degree angle and let the airspeed stabilise. Even relatively small targets could be identified at about 20,000 ft, while appropriate adjustments were made for the final attack in the dive.

'Usually, these attacks came as a total surprise to the enemy, since they were unaware we were even in the area! The first indication of our attack was usually the detonation of our bombs. Very often, the last aircraft had cleared the target before the first round of anti-aircraft fire was noticed.'

Another Ops Officer who enjoyed great success with the bombsight was Maj Ebersole of the 12th FBS;

'I think that the manual pipper control that we had been given after we had been in combat with the Sabres for awhile was one of the best things to happen to us. It helped us improve our accuracy. Famous test pilot Bob Hoover from North American Aviation came over and demonstrated it, using one of our squadron aircraft. Some of our pilots, however, took a grease pencil and a straight edge and put a 45-degree line on the left side of the canopy. Thus, when they were in their dive and that line was on the horizon, they knew that they were exactly 45 degrees off the horizontal! Whatever method was used, we learned to put our bombs squarely on the intended target, and that was why we were there!'

Lt Bob Kibort of the 67th FBS also vividly remembers his bombing experiences with the F-86F;

'The gun/bombsight was essentially the same colli-mated device that had been used by our fighters at the end of World War 2. The main exception was the radar-ranging input (Type A-4), rather than the manual twist of the throttle on the F-86A (Type A-1CM), to control the range input to the computerised firing solution. Initially, the bombsight was a predetermined depression of the gunsight aiming reticule. However, about the time I got to Osan in the spring of 1953, Bob Hoover arrived with his modification. It was basically a series of lines painted on both sides of the canopy which, when aligned with the horizon, produced a specific dive angle. In addition, a small altimeter was added alongside the gunsight, which would trigger a light at a predetermined altitude.

'Because the sight line was depressed, and not aligned with the roll axes of the Sabre, whenever a correction in roll was made during the bomb run, the sight would appear to swing as if it were attached to the end of a pendulum. The effect on a stabilised dive angle was wild, even after getting used to it. You had to be very careful not to get target fixation and make "one last correction" before pull up. I can vividly remember on one mission where I made that "correction" and I pulled well over the 7G load limit when coming off the target. Fortunately, even though the G-meter showed 8+, an inspection of the aircraft after I got back indicated no damage, and it continued to fly.'

There were numerous incidents in which the F-86 withstood G-forces far greater than the manufacturer had recommended. Indeed, it was such a tough fighter that the pilots did not worry about overstressing the airframe in a critical situation. And the F-86F fighter-bomber version was undoubtedly put to the test more often than the interceptor models because of the weighty bombload that it carried. The 12th FBS's Maj Ebersole again;

'I remember one time when I pulled 9G on a bomb run. I was in a steep dive with two 1000-lb bombs on

BELOW DENNIS THE MENACE *has been towed out to the range to have its guns harmonised at Osan in late June 1953. Exactly one year later, the USAF would reach its peak strength in respect to the number of fighter wings it had flying either A-, E- or F-model F-86s. On 30 June 1954, there were no fewer than 19 wings equipped with Sabres, although by 30 June 1955 this total had dropped to 13 (Art Huhn)*

board. I "pickled" both at the same time and neither of them released. It was very difficult to pull the aircraft out of the dive, but I did it without suffering any structural problems. After returning to base, the jet was checked over by the maintenance people, and they could find nothing wrong, so it continued to fly missions.'

If there had been an inherent structural weakness in the Sabre, many pilots would not have lived to talk about it.

While the greatest dangers in the Korean War were faced by the troops in the frontline and the aircrews either supporting them directly, or ranging deep into enemy territory, it wasn't exactly safe to be on the flightline either – especially if your job entailed handling live ordnance, or directly maintaining the aircraft. Explaining the 'lot' of the unsung groundcrewman in Korea is Crew Chief, Sgt Herbert Baer, who was with the 36th FBS when they turned in their F-80Cs for new Sabres. He recalls an

incident on the line at Suwon that could have turned into a disaster;

'Things sometimes get out of hand on an otherwise routine day. I remember one time when an armourer was reloading 0.50-cal ammo into the guns of an F-86F that was parked in the front revetment line. He accidentally charged off a round. It passed under the left wing of the aircraft in front, between the drop tank and a 500-lb bomb, and hit a power unit that was parked in front of the wing. The round pierced the fuel tank of the unit, setting it on fire. The driver of a fuel truck parked alongside a neighbouring Sabre saw the smoke and flames and abandoned his truck for "parts unknown".

'Two airmen brought up a large wheeled fire bottle and unravelled the hose. Upon opening the valve, it was discovered that the bottle was empty! The airmen looked into the nozzle in disbelief and abandoned the area also. A technical sergeant then grabbed the tongue of the

power unit and started to pull it away from the aircraft. However, the cables were still plugged into the F-86 at the rear of the wing. When he got to the end of the slack, the unit bounced back like it was on a rubber band. Finally, he got it unplugged and pulled clear at about the time the alert crash truck arrived and doused everything in sight.

'The whole episode had only taken a couple of minutes, but it looked like a *Keystone Kops* comedy! The technical sergeant got a medal for his action. Fortunately, there was very little damage to the equipment or aircraft, but it could have easily gone the other way.'

FINAL BATTLES

It will never be known exactly how much effort the Chinese put into their ground strategy during the final

weeks of the war. Intelligence during that period was sketchy due to the hidden movements of the enemy at night, and during the day, very few enemy troops were out in the open. They continued to probe until they found a weak spot in the UN frontline, and then they broke through for a about 15 miles, before air power halted the offensive and friendly ground forces drove them back to their original positions. However, there was more to this event than anyone will ever know.

The impact of this offensive on the war, should it have met with success, will never be known, for details were 'hushed up' and the press never briefed on the communist push. There are probably thousands of ex-American military personnel alive today as the result of what 18th FBW Sabres accomplished in the span of a few hours.

On 15 June 1953, 18th FBW Ops Officer, Maj Flamm

BELOW *All dressed up and only one place to go – North Korea. These 36th FBS pilots, suited up and finished with their briefings, are being dropped off on the flightline. Although the weather may have been warm on the ramp, at 40,000 ft things got a little cool in the cockpit – hence the bulky clothing. Evidently, there was a shortage of vehicles at Suwon, for all of the pilots involved in the mission have jumped on this one Jeep! Normally, a truck would have been provided (Dick Seger)*

RIGHT *The camera frames a legend! Lt Col James Hagerstrom, CO of the 67th FBS, was photographed in front of the squadron operations building during the early days of F-86F operations – note the old paint scheme on the vertical fin of the Sabre in the distance. Hagerstrom was the only 'ace' to emerge from the fighter-bomber ranks, and this may have been because his number one priority was to drop his bomb load as quickly as possible and head for 'MiG Alley'! (Don McNamara)*

Harper, found himself in charge of the wing when both his boss and the group commander were away attending a military conference in Japan. During that single day, the wing completed 92 sorties as part of a typical flying schedule. At 1700 hours, the final two flights of Sabres launched on this record-breaking day were still north of the frontline. Having turned for home, the pilots suddenly spotted something that they had rarely seen before. Maj Harper recalls some of the details;

'Just as I thought we were about through for the day, Lt Col Harry Evans, who was leading one of the flights, called in on his radio. He stated that they had just spotted about 100 boxcars in a marshalling yard in close proximity to the frontline. This was very unusual. Evans also stated that when they made firing passes on them, the rail cars erupted with huge secondary explosions. This meant that they were loaded with munitions. Finally, he added that another marshalling yard close by had an equal number of boxcars in it. Evans relayed the target co-ordinates to us, and we set the wheels in motion for an instantaneous response. This was something very big, and

time was definitely not on our side! The 18th was a daylight outfit, and darkness was just about on us.

'We could not reach any one of rank to give us authorisation to initiate a major strike this late in the evening. Something had to be done at once because the boxcars would be unloaded during the night, and there would be nothing left to hit at first light. This would be the toughest decision of my career. While the Combat Operations Center's Duty Officer relayed the "scramble" order and target data to the eight alert aircraft, I contacted Fifth AF Combat Ops Center to give them the co-ordinates of the targets, and tell them what we were planning on doing. Within 15 minutes we launched 16 more F-86s. We also prepared to receive and reload the jets that were already hitting the marshalling yards.

'This ended up being a major wing effort. By now, we were in total darkness and the flights continued. I was informed by both the 12th and 67th FBS commanders that once our aircraft had gotten airborne, the fires from the munitions cache were burning so bright that it was easy to find the target.

BELOW A quartet of Sabre combat veterans pose for the camera. These men are, from left to right, Lt Col Harry 'The Horse' Evans, Maj Carl Lovell, Capt Dennis Clark and Maj Richard Kenney. All were experienced in the 'management' of the 18th FBW's squadrons, and frequently scheduled themselves for missions into the most dangerous areas of North Korea. Their knowledge was duly passed on to the younger generation of pilots that were sent to Korea fresh from training school in early 1953 (Dick Kenney)

'That entire valley was lit up like daylight. The other pilots stated that once they got up to 6000 ft, the fires were like a beacon. We were putting so many aircraft into the target area that it soon became very dangerous for the jets milling around in the darkness. Finally, a C-47 arrived on the scene with a FAC onboard, and he took over directing the attacks.

'We were well into the "surge", and no one on base knew that this operation did not have Fifth AF approval! I was the only one that had this knowledge and it was too late to stop. At one point, I requested that the Combat Ops Center of Fifth AF either get approval or order me to stop the operation. I received neither.

'Shortly after midnight, we lost two aircraft due to ground fire. In view of these losses, I knew that none of this could be kept quiet. Within that 24-hour period, the 18th FBW had generated approximately 212 sorties, of which 120 had not been authorised by the Air Force. We had completely destroyed the Chinese cache of munitions that were to support the "million-man offensive" that never happened.

'None of these figures, or achievements, appeared in any of the wing records, and very little was said about it. The important thing is that the decision was made, we accomplished our objective and thousands of lives were probably saved.'

As a postscript to this incident, the *official* record for sorties in one day remains with the 36th FBS, and historical data still shows that the 18th FBW flew 'just' 92 assigned sorties for that mid-June day, which was perhaps one of the most significant of the whole war.

Lt Charles B Cox of the 36th FBS recalls his involvement in the June Chinese Offensive;

'I can vividly recall the big bombing surge we had in the middle of June. The weather was clear, which was not always the case. The Chinese troops had launched an all-out attack against the RoK forces that were defending part of the frontline – I understand that they punched through 30 or more miles. We were tasked with trying to break-up the offensive, and I remember flying four missions on one of those days.

'These sorties saw us performing a combination of dive-bombing and strafing. We attacked positions that had been on our side of the front, so we had some easily recognisable targets (buildings, bridges, roads etc.). On my third mission of the day, I was flying element lead (the No 3 position) in a flight of four. After my dive-bomb run, I felt the normal release thump, pulled out of the dive and broke into a left climbing turn over enemy lines. This was standard procedure in the event that you had hung bomb(s). The No 4 man called out for me to break hard right – the AAA gunners had zeroed in on me.

'During the climb, I made safe my bomb switch without realising that one of my 1000-lb bombs was hung on the right pylon. When the switch went to the safe position, the hung bomb dropped. My flight leader, Lt Paul Gushwa, went down to see where it had hit, and I followed him. It exploded in an open area devoid of activity.

'This type of accident was our greatest fear – accidentally hitting friendly troops. Upon my return to Suwon AB, we passed the info onto HQ Fifth AF. There were no reports of "friendlies" being hit, so we were relieved. Under normal conditions, we would always be working with a FAC, who would usually mark our targets with "Willie Peter" – white phosphorous rockets. But, under the circumstances of the big Chinese push, we didn't work with one on this mission. It was a very hectic time, and our job was to get as many bombs on the enemy in as short a time as possible. I recall that some of our pilots got in five missions during that single day.'

Unofficial historical records for the 18th FBW show that the 36th FBS alone flew 121 sorties on 15 June, which was an air force record that almost certainly still stands to this day

There has been some speculation as to why napalm wasn't the weapon of choice as it had been during the 18th's Mustang days. The statistics that are mentioned in the recorded microfilm history of the wing during its Sabre days does not reveal the use of napalm during the heavy May/June/July period. Lt. Herbert Schimsk, 35th FBS pilot, sheds some light on this;

'With regard to the F-86F delivering napalm, I guess it could do it as well as the F-80 and F-84. You have to realise that the terrain and rules of engagement were very limiting factors in Korea. In both of the missions where I used napalm, we were required to make runs over enemy territory parallel to the frontline in order to preclude dropping our ordnance on "friendlies". In both cases, ridges and valleys blocked our approaches from either the north or the south, leaving us to run in from either the east or the west, and thus making it impossible to drop effectively from level flight.'

During the last eight months of the war, the relative stability of the frontline could only be determined by jamming as many troops as possible (friendly and enemy) into a very tight area. Therefore, the risk of hitting UN troops proved to be just too great for the use of napalm.

ABOVE When it came to creature comforts in Korea, although the sleeping quarters might have been a little on the austere side, the 'O'Club' was most definitely not – this was the place to be when off duty! Most of the Officer's Clubs that were strung around the various South Korean bases were decorated with excellent murals depicting the wings' history, or more recent accomplishments against the MiGs. The squadron emblems displayed in this photograph relate to the 12th and 67th FBSs (Robert Niklaus)

It is difficult to judge just how much impact the F-86F fighter-bomber had on the war effort once the two wings became fully operational. Only accurate statistics can demonstrate how much destruction and disruption the 8th and 18th FBWs inflicted on the communist forces.

The following figures were taken from microfilm records of the 18th FBW for the April/May/June 1953 period. From these figures, one can easily gauge the momentum that had was built up by the Sabres units at Osan and Suwon: These figures include all three squadrons within the 18th.

STATISTICS FOR THE 18th FBW IN KOREA IN 1953

	APRIL	MAY	JUNE
Average Number of F-86Fs Assigned	45	44	43
Total Hours of Flying Time	1933.25	2054	2211
Average Hours per F-86F	43	47	51
Number of Sorties Flown	623	1234	1606
Percent of F-86Fs in Commission	83%	91%	92%
Total F-86Fs Lost in Combat	0	1	9
Total F-86Fs Lost (other reasons)	0	3	4
Fuel Consumed (Gallons)	819,415	942,069	959,684
Engine Changes	7	4	10
0.50-cal Rounds Expended	23,631	104,780	241,452
Napalm	0	4	56
5-in Rockets Expended	0	0	0
500-lb Bombs	569	982	1038
1000-lb Bombs	0	1116	1434
260-lb 'Frag' Bombs	0	0	0
AN-M76 Incendiary Bombs	0	0	2
Major Inspections	17	25	?
F-86Fs Battle Damaged (Major)	1	1	5.
F-86Fs Battle Damaged (Minor)	0	2	5

The figures contained within this table also accurately reflect the totals for the 8th FBW during the May-June period as well, for both organisations were similarly tasked.

There were a lot of unsung heroes in Korea, and many of them did not come home. The real tragedy of their loss is that today, only their families, and the pilots that served with them, remember their sacrifice. This photo (taken in May 1953) shows Lt Chadwick Smith, who flew with the 12th FBS, preparing for a mission in his assigned F-86F, FU-380. On 15 June he was killed in action while bombing communisat targets in this aircraft (Howard Heiner)

MAIN PICTURE *Despite the fact that the war was still being fought at an increasingly hectic pace, the groundcrew of the 18th FBW still found the time to embellish a number of the the external tanks fitted to Sabres within the wing. This 12th FBS jet, for example, carries tanks detailed in the squadron's familiar yellow colour. These vital external stores were not cheap to manufacture, and fortunately for the fighter-bomber pilots, they were seldom 'punched off' for MiG-15s were rarely encountered by this late stage of the war. The artwork worn by The Stinger was painted on by its crew chief. This photograph was taken as the flight returned home following the completion of a mission (John Dawson)*

INSETS *The emblem above was an unofficial creation inspired by the various flights that formed the 67th FBS, which were all identified by the names of drinks – Coke, rye, gin etc. Fixed above the unit's 'hooch', this sign left no doubt as to who 'lived' there. The second sign is an exact copy of the official 67th FBS patch worn both on pilots' flightsuits and on squadron aircraft (Cliff Nunnery)*

RIGHT *During June 1953 the time spent by aircraft on the ground during daylight hours was kept to a minimum. A high in-service rate was maintained by the 18th FBW, allowing the wing to cope with the sortie 'surges' that punctuated the final weeks of the Korean War. Here, 12th FBS Sabres are being simultaneously serviced, refuelled and bombed up, thus drastically cutting turn around times (John Batchelder)*

KOREAN RECORDS FOR THE 8TH FBW

1. First USAF wing committed to action in Korea

2. First jet wing to see combat

3. First jet wing to shoot down an enemy aircraft

4. First to fly 255 sorties in one day (a record that they later broke)

5. First to fly 290 sorties in one day (15/6/53)

6. First to fly 50,000 sorties in jet warfare (again, they broke their own record, and were the first to fly 60,000 sorties in jet warfare on 30/5/53 – the 8th FBW ended the war with a total of 64,679 sorties flown)

7. Wing's 36th FBS was the first unit to fly 121 combat sorties in one day (15/6/53), a record which still stands

8. Wing dropped 82,1125,000 lbs of explosives during the war

9. Wing flew more combat sorties than any other USAF unit in Korea

These 'first' were taken from the records of Raymond C Lee, who served with the 8th FBW as Wing Operations Officer, and as the 35th FBS's Operations Officer and, finally, as the latter unit's CO.

BELOW *Fighter-bomber ace Maj James Hagerstrom is seen here helping groundcrews ready his Sabre for another mission. His enthusiasm for the 'kill' was reflected in the chances he took 'sneaking up' to the areas frequented by MiG-15s after he had made his bombing run. Hagerstrom was criticised for this more than once, and he almost certainly would have dropped down the ranks to lieutenant if it had meant being able to fly fighter-interceptor missions with the 4th or 51st FIWs once again! Instead, he was promoted to lieutenant-colonel and eventually posted back to the USA (Archie Buie)*

ABOVE *Pilot Lt Kenneth Koon (right) poses with his crew chief prior to a mission. This view shows FU-360 from the left side, revealing one of its nicknames (the Princess). On the right side it wore the legend Pretty Patty. Whilst at Osan, 67th FBS Sabres had their red squadron trim kept in immaculate condition, the groundcrews striving to keep the painted areas chip free (Kenneth Koon)*

ABOVE From this angle FU-360's starboard artwork is clearly visible. Nicknames or nose-art worn on the starboard side of the aircraft was usually chosen by the jet's crew chief, or a member of the ground support crew, whilst the port side was the pilot's domain (Kenneth Koon)

LEFT On many missions flight composition was often mixed, with two jets from one squadron being joined by two from another. Here, a 35th FBS Sabre has pulled up alongside a 36th FBS aircraft en route to Suwon following a bombing strike over North Korea. Sometimes, these combinations resulted from one Sabre aborting a mission and taking his wingman back with him to base as an escort – standard wing policy. This left an element of two Sabres free to join up with others in the formation (Paul Gushwa)

RIGHT *A 67th FBS Sabre flies in close formation with his element lead. With no external fuel tanks showing, this jet has either had to jettison them as a result of combat, or is flying a test 'hop' in the Osan area after routine maintenance. All F-86 wings that were based in South Korea had their major maintenance done in Japan When the war ended in late July 1953, there were a total of 297 Sabres in-theatre. This placed a heavy burden on maintenance personnel, regardless of whether they were based in Japan or in South Korea (Caroll Blum)*

BELOW RIGHT *SWEET SUE of the 12th FBS almost certainly boasted more kill markings than any other Sabre in either FBW. Although this unit failed to produce a single ace, it would seem likely that FU-381 was involved in the destruction of at least two MiGs. The remaining red stars almost certainly denote kills scored by pilots that flew this aircraft after they had enjoyed success with other squadrons. This particular pilot is using a Korean umbrella to ward off the summer sun during his shift on the alert pad at Osan (William Barber)*

BELOW *There was always activity on, and around, the alert pad. Here, HONEY (from the 36th FBS) is undergoing the final phase of preparations prior to it being declared mission capable. The jet's pilot, meanwhile, can be seen standing off the port wingtip, deep in discussion with a fellow aviator. In the immediate aftermath of the ceasefire, all four Sabre wings based in Korea were responsible for furnishing a set number of aircraft for the daily alert duty. Indeed, the F-86 was the only aircraft type in-theatre that had the speed to conduct a successful interception prior to communist jets causing major damage, should they have attempted a surprise attack on the south (Richard Seger)*

RIGHT *Sgt Vic Collier checks that the 1000-lb bombs loaded to 'his' Sabre have been fused correctly. This 67th FBS F-86F was photographed at Osan during the mission 'surge' undertaken by the 18th FBW in the May/June/July 1953 period (Vic Collier)*

FAR RIGHT *Capt Dennis Clark, Operations Officer for the 67th FBS, prepares to start his engine prior to departing on a bombing sortie 'up north'. His assigned aircraft was* DENNIS THE MENACE, *which was duly re-allocated to Lt Reid Ivins when Clark completed his tour in Korea (Kenneth Koon)*

BOTTOM RIGHT *Lt Jack Cook's* DELTA QUEEN II *(FU-379) is seen parked on the flightline at Suwon during the summer of 1953 (Jack Cook)*

RIGHT *All of the 8th FBW's squadrons were obligated to 'pull' their share of alert duty, as shown here. Facing the 36th FBS pilot/ photographer across the alert pad is a 35th FBS F-86F. Ground support personnel were never far away in case the klaxon sounded, scrambling the aircraft (Jack Taylor)*

BELOW RIGHT *Traditionally, the most colourful Sabre in the 8th FBW was the personal mount of the wing commander. And despite lacking nose-art or a nickname, the multi- coloured bands around the forward fuselage and colourful fin sunburst made the Sabre stand out from all the others on the flightline (U B Alford)*

LEFT *Capt Jack Magee (centre) of the 36th FBS celebrates his 100th mission with his crew chief and another groundcrew- man. Magee's aircraft during his tour of duty bore the name KATHRYN II in honour of his wife. This photograph was taken at Suwon during the summer of 1953 (Jack Magee)*

BELOW LEFT *On a rare 'off day', it was easy to round up a few pilots (suitably adorned in appropriately coloured scarves and ball caps, of course) to pose for some pictures out on the flightline. This shot was taken in the spring of 1953, prior to the onset of the heavy sortie 'surges' that were required to counter the Chinese ground offensives. The 12th FBS Sabre that serves as the backdrop for this shot (FU-323) was lost on a combat mission on 16 June 1953 whilst being flown by Lt James Allston (William Barber)*

RIGHT *This early morning view of the flightline at Suwon reveals the activity and preparation involved in changing shifts on the alert pad. Note that all the survival gear for each pilot has been placed neatly on the wing of* MRS CATHY. *Most of the alert responsibility for Suwon during the war years was shouldered by the 51st FIW (Dick Seger)*

ABOVE Shimpai Nai *was a 36th FBS Sabre flown by Lt Jack Taylor, who had earlier completed a significant number of missions in the F-80C, before converting to the F-86F. Within a 34-month period, the 36th had begun the war flying F-80Cs, switched over to the F-51D for several months, and then reverted back to the F-80C. Finally, in early 1953 they converted onto the F-86F (Jack Taylor)*

In the process of setting many bombing records during the summer of 1953, both the 8th and 18th FBWs lost their fair share of aircraft and pilots. Seen here surveying the aftermath of one such crash on 31 May 1953 is Capt Bill Juhrs (right), who was the Flying Safety Officer for the 18th FBW. He is surrounded by the wreckage of a 12th FBS F-86F, which crashed near the frontline after its pilot, Lt. Marion Smotherman, became disoriented in bad weather and flew straight into the ground. The crash site was close to a US Army position, which allowed the two officers access to the remains of the Sabre (Bill Juhrs)

Photographed at Suwon AB on the 80th FBS's flightline, the pilot of this Sabre patiently waits for the fuel truck and bomb crew to finish up so that he can get on with his mission. The ordnance load carried by his Sabre comprises two 1000-lb GP bombs, which are destined for a target in the extreme northern sectors of North Korea (Robert Odle)

CHAPTER 5

POSTWAR ACTIVITIES IN KOREA

BELOW *Lt Joel Perry has a last-minute discussion with his crew chief, prior to undertaking a test hop in his F-86F in the wake of a routine maintenance period. This photograph was taken in the autumn of 1953, several months after the war had ended. By this stage, the only 18th FBW Sabres loaded with ordnance were the jets sat on the alert pad. Although the fighting was now technically over, pilots still accumulated plenty of flying time on sorties flown south of the 38th Parallel (Robert Hook)*

When the ceasefire came into effect on 27 July 1953, both the American public and media alike considered the Korean War over. However, for the men of the four Sabre wings in-theatre, the conflict was far from over. Indeed, the situation in North and South Korea has changed very little over the past 46 years, with both countries still remaining sworn enemies.

The F-86 wings remained on-station for over a year, and there were numerous MiG kills made during this time. With the threat of conflict never far away, it was essential that the new Sabre pilots that rotated into South Korea in 1954 had honed their air-to-air combat skills prior to their arrival. The 4th FIW remained at Kimpo until 1 October 1954, when it finally moved its operation to Chitose AB, Japan, whilst the 51st FIW stayed at Suwon until 1 August 1954. At that time, the famous 'checker tails' moved to Naha AB, on Okinawa.

The two fighter-bomber wings also had plans to pull out after four years on Korean soil. The 8th FBW was the first to leave, returning to its old base at Itazuke in October 1954. That left the 18th FBW as the last USAF F-86 wing in South Korea, and it would take up residence at Kadena AB, also on Okinawa, on 1 November 1954. Today, the F-15C Eagle-equipped 18th FW still remains at Kadena as one of the most formidable combat outfits in the USAF's arsenal. The Sabre legend in Korea itself would be passed on to the 58th FW at Osan in March 1955.

Right after the war ended, there was a mass exodus

LEFT *Both the 8th and 18th FBWs had colourful patches made up for their individual flights. Here, Lt Frank Harrison of the 12th FBS shows off his 'Dog Flight' patch, along with the unit's 'Foxy Few' emblem, which was standard for the entire squadron. The yellow building in the background is the squadron's Operations shack, these buildings often being painted in the colours of their respective unit. This photo was taken in the spring of 1953 at Osan (Frank Harrison)*

of experienced F-86 pilots. Realising that all four wings could be left well short of seasoned personnel, the FEAF ordered extensions to some of the pilots' tours, thus giving units ample time to train new pilots. 2Lt James Carter was one of the replacements that had rotated into South Korea several months after the war, joining the 35th FBS. Here, he remembers those days;

'Most of the experienced pilots that had some combat time were already gone when I arrived. Our training received top priority. During this period, the 8th FBW was on a three-day rotating squadron schedule: one day on air defence alert (12 aircraft in total, with four on two-minute alert, four on five-minute alert and four on 15-minute alert); the next day on "frag" alert (most aircraft bombed up and on standby); and the final day spent training. The latter saw us conduct air-to-air banner gunnery, air-to-ground gunnery on controlled ranges, and live ordnance drops using 250-, 500- and 1000-lb bombs. We dropped them on a small island out in the Yellow Sea.

'Later in my tour the wing moved back to Japan. By this time I had made 1st Lieutenant, and was a flight leader. The 8th still maintained its obligation in South Korea. We would go back TDY, and fly a set number of Yalu patrols. I was involved in two of these. The first one was to Kimpo (K-14) and the second to Kunsan (K-8). One of these times, the 335th FIS was TDY out of Osan.

'Between the two squadrons, we handled all of the flights up the coast and back. I can recall one day when the 335th was up and got jumped by several MiG-15s.

ABOVE *Fighter pilots, as a whole, are the same the world over – they fight hard and party hard. This picture was taken in October 1953 at the Officers' Club at Osan, by which time the cool autumn weather had already arrived. Two squadron emblems are visible in this shot, the pilot in the middle of the photo having a large 67th FBS 'Fighting Cock' patch sewn onto his jacket, whilst the individual second from the right boasts a 35th FBS 'Black Panthers' emblem on his A-1. The latter pilot must have been visiting Osan, for his squadron normally operated out of Suwon with the 8th FBW (Robert Niklaus)*

LEFT *'Fighting Cocks' to the fore. This shot, taken in October 1953, shows a flight of 67th FBS F-86Fs patrolling off the coast of North Korea. The only time MiG-15s came close to the Sabres during this period was when the latter jets were escorting RB-45 photo-recce aircraft (Robert Niklaus)*

ABOVE *In the weeks after the ceasefire came into effect, both the 8th and 18th FBWs were instructed to put a lot of Sabres into the air to undertake lengthy patrols along both coasts, and immediately below the 38th Parallel. Although the jets carried no bombs, their presence was a show of both force and readiness. Some of the best air-to-air photography was taken at this time, as much formation flying was done in relatively 'relaxed' conditions. These yellow-trimmed F-86Fs of the 12th FBS were photographed in August 1953 (Robert Hook)*

That day I was on alert as leader of a four-ship flight. As soon as the F-86s announced that they had engaged the MiGs, we were scrambled. We were vectored north over the coast past the DMZ, where we met the returning Yalu patrol. Our orders were to engage any MiGs that were following the 335th aircraft, but alas, it was all over, as the enemy fighters chose not to pursue them – probably because the 335th had downed two of them in the fight.'

Lt Robert Niklaus was also involved in a few of these patrols whilst assigned to the 18th FBW in late 1953. One of the missions he recalls here was far more significant than anyone knew at the time, and it proved to be an omen of things to come during the long, drawn out, Cold War that followed the Korean conflict;

'The only good thing about being in Korea was its close proximity to Japan! Our flying time was cut back to about six hours a month, and ever increasing restrictions and supervision virtually eliminated one of our favourite sports, "Sampan Buzzing", as well as the occasional dogfight with our air-to-air neighbours at K-13 and K-14. In the fall of 1953, the "powers that be" decided that we needed to fly off the coast of North Korea all the way up to the mouth of the Yalu River – the precise reason for this was never relayed to us.

'On one such flight, as a relatively junior pilot, I found myself flying the No 2 slot as we passed over the mouth of the Yalu. This meant that when we made the turn back south, my position temporarily put me in the lead of the flight, with the three remaining Sabres crossing behind me. Whilst we were undertaking this manoeuvre, I glanced up ahead and was stunned to see a dozen MiGs heading directly for us! Not only were we in a bad flight position, but we were also somewhat outnumbered. Lead was not eager to be a postwar ace and/or a PoW, so I immediately yelled for us to stick our noses down and head south at maximum speed. These MiGs hung with us about two miles astern all the way down to Chodo Island before breaking off. What we later found out shocked us!

'They were almost certainly new MiG-17s, recently supplied by the Soviet Union. Our engagement with them was probably the first time that they had been sighted in the Far East by the USAF, and that explained why they were able to match our speed, pacing us in the dive. If we had had to "mix it up" with them, it certainly would have been interesting!'

Amongst the young pilots that rotated into Osan a year after the war had ended was 2Lt Vilas Bielefeldt, who was assigned to the 67th FBS. At this time, the 18th FBW's move to Okinawa was close at hand;

'By the end of October 1954, following a heavy schedule, the 18th FBW was in a rather bad way. Parts and supplies were becoming scarce – the civilians back home were sick of war, and did not particularly care about the military, and its lack of proper funding. On more than one patrol, I can recall that some of the cockpit gauges were not working, and I flew a few missions with no exhaust gas temperature registering. I

also remember aborting missions before getting airborne, or even "cranked up". The lack of funding got even worse as we neared our move to Kadena on 30 November.

'At about this time, there were more new pilots coming onboard, and the check-out programme was not really up to scratch – as the following accident reveals. One of the "new heads" was scheduled to tow a banner target (a 6 ft × 30 ft piece of plastic mesh) on the end of a 500-ft cable which was to be used for aerial gunnery training. It became obvious that he had never target-towed before when he asked another pilot how this was done. The latter replied, "Just pull the nose up a bit higher on take-off and leave it on the ground a little longer".

'Well, the Sabre, like any other fighter, will be "behind the power curve" when the nose is raised too high, and despite accelerating well past its take-off speed to about 175 knots, it will never leave the ground! As the aircraft neared the end of the runway, the young pilot figured there was a malfunction with his jet and he was going to

ABOVE *In the last week of July 1953, with the cease-fire just days old, the F-86 wings commenced dawn and dusk patrols off both coasts. This 67th FBS Sabre was photographed at first light returning to Osan, via the west coast of Korea, in September 1953. MiGs were rarely encountered during this period, although clashes became more commonplace in 1954 (Robert Niklaus)*

RIGHT Suited up in typical attire for a Sabre pilot in Korea in 1953, Lt Robert Niklaus is seen ready to climb into his jet on the alert pad at Osan AB in November of that year. Niklaus was one of several pilots who recorded much of the F-86F's history with his 35 mm camera, loaded with Kodachrome 25 film. Behind him is L Carroll Baird's assigned Sabre. The 18th FBW would eventually move from Korea to Okinawa in late 1954, where the wing remains to this day (Robert Niklaus)

FAR RIGHT Maj Raymond Lee, CO of the 35th FBS, was photographed immediately after he had returned from a patrol along the coast of Korea. This shot was taken in early September 1953 at Suwon, which remained the home of the 8th FBW until it moved back to Japan (Raymond Lee) have to eject. As he let go of the stick, the aircraft's nose dropped and it began to fly, but by this stage there was no one at the controls, for the pilot had already initiated the ejection sequence. The F-86 started to roll, and when at 90 degrees of bank, the pilot "punched out" – by this time he was parallel with the ground. The jet nosed in and blew up, and the crash truck was soon on the scene.

'The rescue crew proceeded to wade through the flames to get the pilot out, for they had not seen him eject. To their astonishment, the pilot instead staggered out of a rice paddy, which had probably saved his life. A mass-briefing on tow procedures was duly conducted!'

The Sabre was a 'major player' within the USAF in the Far East from 1951 through to 1957, after which time the F-100 assumed its duties. The presence of the F-86F on Korean soil lasted much longer than anyone could have imagined, for the 58th FW 'carried the banner' in the wake of the four main combat wings until July 1958, when it moved back to CONUS. The wing's F-86Fs remained in-country, however, for they were passed on to the RoKAF.

FAR LEFT TOP *This polished silver Sabre doesn't have nose art or a name, but it does have command stripes, signifying that it was flown by the squadron boss – in this case, Maj Raymond Lee, who led the 35th FBS immediately postwar (Raymond Lee)*

FAR LEFT BOTTOM *2Lt Bill Gries prepares to 'light the burners' on his Hoosier Hotshot. His crew chief can be seen holding the seat harness straps aloft whilst Gries get comfortable in his 'office'. This photograph was taken in the autumn of 1953 at Osan. During the final two months of the war, the 18th FBW was involved in over a thousand immediate close support missions. These were not pre-planned, the aircraft instead being called in by an airborne FAC to render quick assistance to friendly troops under fire (Robert Niklaus)*

LEFT *Lt Joseph Lynch has donned all of his flight gear and is ready to climb into the cockpit of his 35th FBS Sabre. Note the large 'Black Panther' patch sewn onto his jacket. Lt Lynch was involved in numerous post-war patrols off the coast of North Korea, where he frequently escorted reconnaissance jets into communist airspace, or escorted the aircraft out of harm's way upon the completion of their mission. The majority of these sorties were assigned to the 4th and 51st FIWs, however (Joe Lynch)*

RIGHT *Rapidly approaching the no-fly zone close to the 38th Parallel, the pilot of this 67th FBS Sabre begins to turn south back towards his base at Osan. This photograph was taken in September 1953 (Robert Niklaus)*

BELOW *Lt James Carter's My Sweetie is shown parked in the area at Suwon where aircraft were 'hosed down and cleaned up'. The blue sunburst on the tail was the 35th FBS's wing marking, whilst the 80th FBS used yellow, as seen on the aircraft parked in the background. When the 8th FBW pulled back to Japan in late 1954, the 80th FBS stayed behind to assist the 58th FW in its transition from F-84s to F-86s at Taegu AB (K-2) (James Carter)*

FAR LEFT *Lt Vilas Bielfeldt poses with his crew chief prior to taxying out on a another routine postwar sortie from Osan. The former was with the 67th FBS when the wing made the long move to Okinawa. On that day in November 1954, a total of 70 Sabres and three T-33s launched for the brief flight to Itazuke, where they all refuelled, and then pressed on over water to Kadena (Vilas Bielfeldt)*

LEFT TOP *A colourful group of 36th FBS pilots gather around Maj Thielhorn's* Rosalie *for a photo session. Note the large 'Flight' emblems that have been sewn onto the pilots' jackets. The squadron was known for its bright red trim and the 'Flying Fiends' badge. Only a few of the pilots seen in this shot – taken in the autumn of 1953 – had flown combat prior to the summer. The 8th FBW was still based at Suwon at the time this shot was taken (Les Sundt)*

LEFT BOTTOM *This 80th FBS Sabre pulls out of its revetment at Suwon just as the sun has begun to set. This aircraft would have been part of a four-ship flight launched to perform the wing's final coastal patrol of the day (Roy Degan)*

RIGHT TOP *In the days immediately following the ceasefire, both FBWs received replacement F-86Fs so as to ensure that all six squadrons in-theatre had their full complement of Sabres. This is well illustrated by this photograph, which features no fewer than 18 35th FBS 'blue tails'. The wing commander's multi-coloured Sabre can also been seen to the left of the shot, whilst the aircraft closest to the camera is F-86F-30 FU-481. As this view clearly shows, despite Suwon being one of the most modern USAF bases in Korea, its parking area contained revetments still 'paved' with PSP (James Setterberg)*

RIGHT BOTTOM *With the war over and the border firmed up, facilities that had been on the temporary side between 1950-53 were drastically improved in early 1954 – as this shot of the 8th FBW's Officers' Club at Suwon clearly shows. Needless to say, this became one of the RoKAF's most desired bases once the USAF pulled out. Although not retaining a permanent presence at Suwon after late 1954, numerous fighter wings deployed from Japan during 1955-56 (James Carter)*

FAR RIGHT *I Mission MARY was a 35th FBS Sabre that bore well-weathered command stripes just forward of its cockpit. The jet's assigned pilot was Capt R N Kelley, who bestowed upon it the name The Jelly Bean. This photograph was taken during the postwar months at Suwon, prior to the 8th FBW moving back to Japan (Marvin Patton)*

RIGHT *Only those that have endured a tour of South Korea during the winter months can attest to the bitter weather conditions faced by groundcrews on the flightline over the decades. This photograph was taken in December 1953 during a typical snow storm for that time of year. Such conditions would have made flying impossible, even if communist forces had been spilling over the 38th Parallel. These F-86Fs belong to the 80th FBS at Suwon AB (Bob McDermott)*

North American F-86F-30 Sabre

1 Radome
2 Radar antenna
3 Engine air intake
4 Gun camera
5 Nosewheel leg doors
6 Nose undercarriage leg strut
7 Aft-retracting nosewheel
8 Torque scissor links
9 Steering control valve
10 Nosewheel leg pivot mounting
11 Sight amplifier
12 Radio and electronics equipment bay
13 Electronics bay access hatch
14 Battery
15 Gun muzzle blast troughs
16 Oxygen bottles
17 Nosewheel bay door
18 Oxygen servicing point
19 Canopy switches
20 Machine gun barrel mountings
21 Hydraulic system test connections
22 Radio transmitter
23 Cockpit armoured bulkhead
24 Armoured glass windscreen panel
25 A-4 gunsight
26 Instrument panel shroud
27 Instrument panel
28 Control column
29 Kick-in boarding step
30 Cartridge case collector box
31 Ammunition magazines, 267 rounds per gun
32 Ammunition feed chutes
33 0.5-in (12.7 mm) Colt-Browning machine guns
34 Engine throttle lever

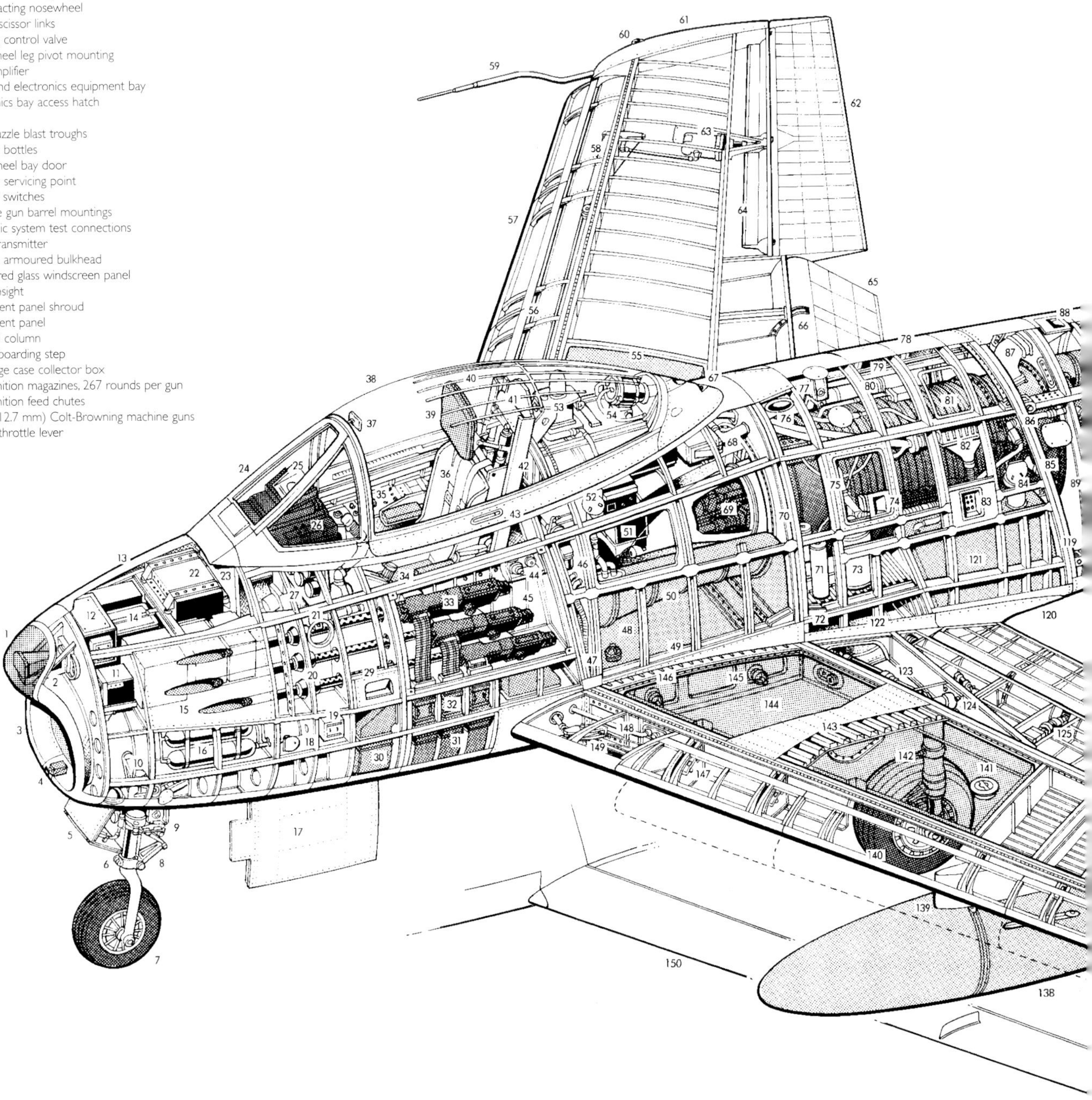

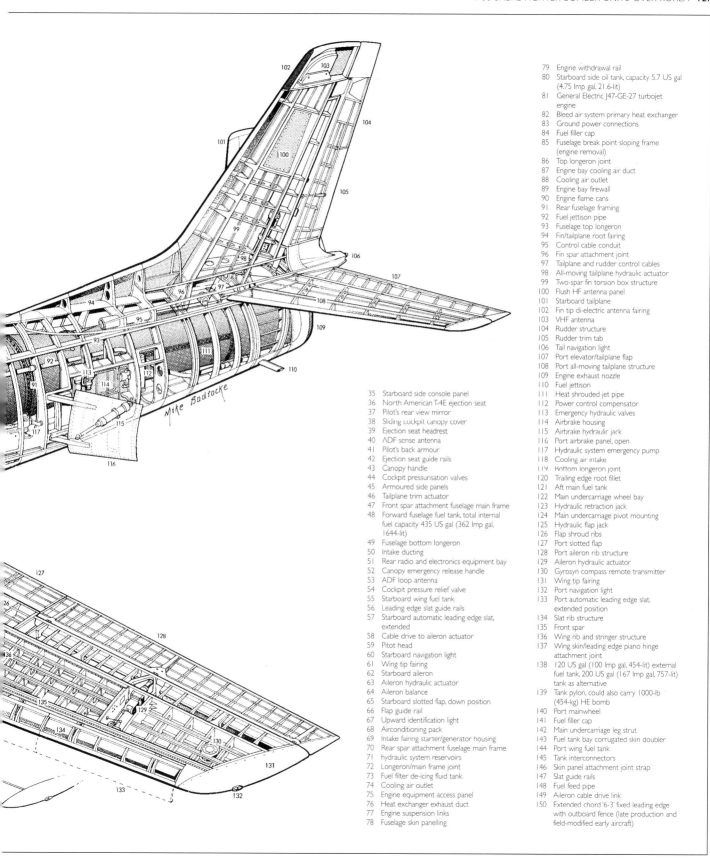

79 Engine withdrawal rail
80 Starboard side oil tank, capacity 5.7 US gal
    (4.75 Imp gal, 21.6-lit)
81 General Electric J47-GE-27 turbojet
    engine
82 Bleed air system primary heat exchanger
83 Ground power connections
84 Fuel filler cap
85 Fuselage break point sloping frame
    (engine removal)
86 Top longeron joint
87 Engine bay cooling air duct
88 Cooling air outlet
89 Engine bay firewall
90 Engine flame cans
91 Rear fuselage framing
92 Fuel jettison pipe
93 Fuselage top longeron
94 Fin/tailplane root fairing
95 Control cable conduit
96 Fin spar attachment joint
97 Tailplane and rudder control cables
98 All-moving tailplane hydraulic actuator
99 Two-spar fin torsion box structure
100 Flush HF antenna panel
101 Starboard tailplane
102 Fin tip di-electric antenna fairing
103 VHF antenna
104 Rudder structure
105 Rudder trim tab
106 Tail navigation light
107 Port elevator/tailplane flap
108 Port all-moving tailplane structure
109 Engine exhaust nozzle
110 Fuel jettison
111 Heat shrouded jet pipe
112 Power control compensator
113 Emergency hydraulic valves
114 Airbrake housing
115 Airbrake hydraulic jack
116 Port airbrake panel, open
117 Hydraulic system emergency pump
118 Cooling air intake
119 Bottom longeron joint
120 Trailing edge root fillet
121 Aft main fuel tank
122 Main undercarriage wheel bay
123 Hydraulic retraction jack
124 Main undercarriage pivot mounting
125 Hydraulic flap jack
126 Flap shroud ribs
127 Port slotted flap
128 Port aileron rib structure
129 Aileron hydraulic actuator
130 Gyrosyn compass remote transmitter
131 Wing tip fairing
132 Port navigation light
133 Port automatic leading edge slat,
    extended position
134 Slat rib structure
135 Front spar
136 Wing rib and stringer structure
137 Wing skin/leading edge piano hinge
    attachment joint
138 120 US gal (100 Imp gal, 454-lit) external
    fuel tank, 200 US gal (167 Imp gal, 757-lit)
    tank as alternative
139 Tank pylon, could also carry 1000-lb
    (454-kg) HE bomb
140 Port mainwheel
141 Fuel filler cap
142 Main undercarriage leg strut
143 Fuel tank bay corrugated skin doubler
144 Port wing fuel tank
145 Tank interconnectors
146 Skin panel attachment joint strap
147 Slat guide rails
148 Fuel feed pipe
149 Aileron cable drive link
150 Extended chord '6-3' fixed leading edge
    with outboard fence (late production and
    field-modified early aircraft)

35 Starboard side console panel
36 North American T-4E ejection seat
37 Pilot's rear view mirror
38 Sliding cockpit canopy cover
39 Ejection seat headrest
40 ADF sense antenna
41 Pilot's back armour
42 Ejection seat guide rails
43 Canopy handle
44 Cockpit pressurisation valves
45 Armoured side panels
46 Tailplane trim actuator
47 Front spar attachment fuselage main frame
48 Forward fuselage fuel tank, total internal
    fuel capacity 435 US gal (362 Imp gal,
    1644-lit)
49 Fuselage bottom longeron
50 Intake ducting
51 Rear radio and electronics equipment bay
52 Canopy emergency release handle
53 ADF loop antenna
54 Cockpit pressure relief valve
55 Starboard wing fuel tank
56 Leading edge slat guide rails
57 Starboard automatic leading edge slat,
    extended
58 Cable drive to aileron actuator
59 Pitot head
60 Starboard navigation light
61 Wing tip fairing
62 Starboard aileron
63 Aileron hydraulic actuator
64 Aileron balance
65 Starboard slotted flap, down position
66 Flap guide rail
67 Upward identification light
68 Airconditioning pack
69 Intake fairing starter/generator housing
70 Rear spar attachment fuselage main frame
71 hydraulic system reservoirs
72 Longeron/main frame joint
73 Fuel filter de-icing fluid tank
74 Cooling air outlet
75 Engine equipment access panel
76 Heat exchanger exhaust duct
77 Engine suspension links
78 Fuselage skin panelling

North American F-86F-30 Sabre

Powerplant

General Electric J47-GE-27 turbojet

Dimensions

Wing Span - 37.12 ft
Length - 37.54 ft
Height - 14.74 ft
Track - 8.3 ft
Wing area - 37.12 ft^2
Aileron area - 16.36 ft^2 each (movement of 15 degrees up/down)
Flap area - 32.51 ft^2
Tail stabiliser area - 19.10 ft^2 (span - 12.75 ft)
Elevator area - 8.62 ft^2 each
Fin area - 25.32 ft^2
Rudder area - 8.12 ft^2
Basic mission wing loading - 59.4 lbs per square feet at 17,921 lbs for take-off

Weight

Empty - 10,890 lbs
Take-off with two 200-gal tanks - 17,921 lbs
Take-off with two 200-gal tanks and two 1000-lb bombs - 20,357 lbs

Fuel

Fuel used - JP4
Internal tanks - 437 gallons
Two drop tanks - 200-gal each

Performance

Take-off stalling speed (power off) - 144 mph (125 knots)
Ground run at sea level - 3320 ft
Distance to clear 50 ft - 4720 ft
Landing ground roll - 2300 ft
Ferry range - 1615 miles (1403 nautical miles)
Combat radius - 458 miles (398 nautical miles)
Average cruising speed - 520 mph (452 knots)
Average cruising speed with two 1000-lb bombs - 486 mph (422 knots)
Maximum speed - 695 mph (604 knots) at sea level, 608 mph (528 knots) at 35,000 ft
Combat radius with two 1000-lb bombs - 316 miles (275 nautical miles)
Total mission time - 2.13 hours
Maximum rate of climb - 9300 ft per minute at sea level
Service ceiling - 48,000 ft